SAVING OUR WORLD FROM
TRUMP

SAVING OUR WORLD FROM **TRUMP**

For information, address Mort Rosenblum: mort.rosenblum@gmail.com

ISBN: 978-1-7355963-1-0 U.S.A.

Published by Old Croc Chronicles, Tucson, AZ

Cover and book design: Gilman Design, Larkspur, CA

Cartoons on pages 50, 74, 95, 129, 175 copyright Jeff Danziger, Washington Post News Service, www.danzigercartoons.com.

*Views expressed in this book are those of author and
do not reflect those of image sources or creators.*

Cover image, courtesy of author.
p. 7   – Trump grafitti / istock.com
p. 12   – "Free Press", Dawn Shepherd
p. 19   – "Any Functioning Adult" sign, photo by Mort Rosenblum
p. 27   – Glen Canyon Dam, Tuxyso / Wikimedia Commons / CC BY-SA 3.0
p. 35   – Sana'a, Yemen, اليدياني / CC BY 3.0
p. 46   – Self Isolation; www.vperemen.com / CC BY SA.
p. 57   – "Homeland Security" sign, photo by Mort Rosenblum
p 67   – Cactus, photo by Mort Rosenblum
p 84   – Trump and Macron shaking hands G7 summit 2018
            Shealah Craighead/ Flickr, The White House on Flickr, public domain
p 134   – Putin and Trump, Kremlin.ru / CC BY SA 4.0
p 137   – Ilhan Omar, Lorie Shaull / CC BY SA 4.0
p 163   – Donald Trump, The White House from Washington, DC /
            2019 National Christmas Tree Lighting Ceremony
p 173   – Dump Trump!, Alisdare Hickson, Canterbury, UK / CC BY-SA 2.0
p 179   – Mort Rosenblum, courtesy of author

For so many who risk so much
trying to get truth to people
who just want a better world.

Contents

A Prior Word

AMERICA'S FIRST PRESIDENT, as the story goes, declared: "I cannot tell a lie." Its forty-fifth will be remembered for the flipside of that: "I cannot tell the truth." In fact, a biographer made up that cherry tree story. All politicians lie to some extent, and a reporter's job is to catch them at it. But Donald Trump is straight out of the *Mein Kampf* playbook. At first, his preposterous repeated lies were almost amusing. Now, as Covid-19 runs wild, they are killing Americans by the scores of thousands. And that is not the half of it.

At home, Trump's depredations, corrupting democracy into authoritarian autocracy, are blindingly clear. But few Americans notice how his self-focused nonpolicy abroad creates conflicts ready to burst into flame. Alternate toadying and bullying have turned China into a bitter adversary intent on reshaping the world in its own repressive image. Stubborn denial of irrefutable evidence thwarts global cooperation to slow a headlong trajectory toward the point where Earth can no longer support human life.

I've been a foreign correspondent since the Associated Press sent me to Africa in 1967. In 1979, I left AP to edit the *International Herald Tribune* in Paris, owned in large part by the *New York Times* and *Washington Post*. In 1981, I rejoined AP with free rein to cover major stories around the world and important ones too slow-moving for big headlines.

The advantage of "mainstream" reporting is earned credibility. You're toast if you slant a story. But it only lets you nudge readers in what you see is the right direction. We lost decades in confronting climate change because reporters balanced scientific fact with self-serving denials from "the other side." I left AP in 2005 to say things as I see them.

These selected pieces are from the *Mort Report*, a back-pocket news agency for people who want it straight. Its editors are colleagues I've learned to trust on the road. We call it non-prophet journalism. It is non-profit, kept going by readers' generosity; no one earns a salary.

And it doesn't prophesize. Dispatches are firsthand reporting, with solid sources and context based on fifty years of covering war and peace on seven continents.

I am a reporter, not an activist. But these dispatches are directed at people who are. Margaret Mead, who thought far beyond her anthropological work on sex in the South Seas, said it well: "Never doubt that a small group of thoughtful, committed, citizens can change the world. Indeed, it is the only thing that ever has."

Trump and his immutable hard core are capable of anything to maneuver their way to an Electoral College win. Democrats, independents and sensible Republicans must deliver a thundering humiliating landslide in November. Eligible voters need to register and not squander a ballot on a third-party candidate in the most crucial election in history.

Find us at **www.mortreport.org**. It is free but all support is appreciated. Please sign up, spread the word and, if you can in these tough times, chip in. Dispatches range widely from around the globe; some are lighthearted, more are hard-edged. These are about Trump. Imagine an America—and a world—after four more years of an unhinged megalomaniac, with a rubberstamp Senate, packed courts and nothing to lose.

These pieces are grouped into five sections. The first were cautionary, written as 2016 elections approached. Recent ones are in the second section, from August 2020 in reverse chronological order. In the third, dispatches from Europe show the global impact of "America First." The fourth section is an essay, a framework around the mosaic, looking upward at the promise of something better. Some miscellany follows.

I. WE SAW IT COMING

A Final Plea

OCTOBER 30, 2016, SINGAPORE – On this crazy-rich fantasy island at the edge of a roiling South China Sea, surrounded by a quarter billion increasingly less moderate Muslims, the stakes are plain. After Nov. 8, our wobbling planet could begin falling on its axis.

Spin the globe, and you find dizzyingly complex crises anywhere it stops. This is no time for a thin-skinned, truth-averse amateur in the White House or a partisan Congress ready to cripple a noble nation for petty narrow interests.

This is a final plea from out in the real world. Vote and get others to vote. Convince fence sitters and third-party people that a ballot for anyone but Hillary Clinton means voting for Trump. Give her the legislative majority she needs.

As we Americans obsess on domestic issues, everyone else watches aghast. A clueless buffoon who denies climate science and rattles a nuclear-tipped saber wants to exchange diplomacy for arm-twisting "deals" that lead to hostilities.

We call our baseball classic the World Series, but we are hardly the world. "They"—everyone but us—total 95.6 percent of it. The European Union is richer than we are. China outnumbers us four to one. Russia matches us nuke for nuke.

"Friend" means less in statecraft than it does on Facebook. Each nation has interests to protect and priorities to balance. Our big guns are no defense against cyber assault. Our drones swell the ranks of ragtag suicidal terrorist groups.

Teddy Roosevelt, a Republican of blessed memory, had it right: If you speak softly, there is no need to demonstrate the heft of your stick.

Our power comes from the fast-dwindling belief that we are committed to trying to do the right thing.

Take Southeast Asia. Jill Stein, the Green candidate, knows about
Aleppo, unlike Gary Johnson, the Libertarian, but she says the South
China Sea is Beijing's private property. In fact, its potential for global
calamity outweighs the Middle East.

Vietnam, our erstwhile enemy, needs help to stare down a looming
China to its north. A new Philippine president who is as loopy as
Trump calls us losers and pledges allegiance to Beijing. So far, he is still
flip-flopping. If he bans U.S. ships from Subic Bay or warplanes from
Clark Air Base, we are toothless in the region.

Singapore fears terror attacks from Indonesia and is wary of China's
claims to crucial international waters. As its booming economy starts
to sputter in a global slowdown, it is keeping its options open.

**We desperately need to dial down rhetoric and filter out bullshit. Yet
Trump does just the opposite. Those still with him are beyond reason.
The more paranoid and preposterous he gets, the louder they cheer.**

To the north, Japan juggles contingencies. And North Korea is the
wildest card in the deck. If Kim Jong-un decides to go out with a bang,
a submarine-launched missile on a U.S.-flagged Pacific base is enough
to trigger a proper World War Three.

If this doesn't worry you, consider Russia. Vladimir Putin can freeze
Europe in winter simply by shutting off the gas. We really don't need
a game of chicken at the eastern edges of a NATO that Trump disparages. Then, of course, there is Syria.

The main Trump card, outrageously exploited, is immigration. For this,
Southeast Asia is instructive. We trashed Vietnam but at least took in
many of the refugees we created. Today, 1.4 million Vietnamese season
our melting pot.

In the last debate, Trump said hundreds of thousands of Syrians have flooded our shores. The actual total is near 10,000, all intensely screened. Germany, which opposed the war that produced so many refugees, has resettled more than a million.

Refugees are victims, not terrorists. Most have skills to start enterprises that add jobs rather than take them away. But the key argument for generosity is self-serving. Abandoning people to dead-end desperation breeds murderous hatred.

The rap against Mexicans is bad faith or ignorance. More now leave than arrive. A Wall, however high, won't stop suppliers who satisfy our drug habit. Fairer trade, smarter aid, temporary work permits are better answers.

In Singapore, Kishore Mahbubani, former U.N. ambassador who now heads the Lee Kuan Yew School of Public Policy at the national university, worries not only about Trump but also about America in general. "We defend human rights better than you do," he told me. "You torture, we don't."

What is wrong with this picture?

Singapore flogs minor offenders until they pass out from pain, and there is much else to say on this subject. But we may elect a man who thinks waterboarding is a bare minimum, a punishment terror suspects deserve on general principles.

We desperately need to dial down rhetoric and filter out bullshit. Yet Trump does just the opposite. Those still with him are beyond reason. The more paranoid and preposterous he gets, the louder they cheer.

Imagine Trump in the Situation Room, not CNN's but the real one. He mocks the generals for signaling the Mosul assault. A "sneak attack" would have trapped Islamic State leaders inside the city.

Anyone who didn't dodge the draft can tell you the inevitable result, even if commanders could have masked the buildup of 100,000 coalition troops. But here's a report from David Kilcullen, an Australian colonel who advised David Petraeus.

"A rapid attack was always out of the question, given the huge size of Mosul, the deep collapse of Iraqi forces in 2014…and suffering and subsequent crisis that shook Iraqi society to its core.

"Likewise, as emotionally satisfying as it might be to carpet-bomb Mosul, the civilian casualties this would entail, and the destruction of one of Iraq's great urban and cultural centres, would be ethically and legally unacceptable."

Bombing a city creates rubble and cratered roads. Defenders emerge from shelters and dig in for prolonged siege. Forcing ISIS leaders onto open desert makes them easy targets with limited "collateral damage."

Taking Mosul matters, but ISIS will survive. Trump would have flattened a 5,000-year-old city with a million civilians trapped inside to no practical effect. Global reaction would have fueled incalculable rancor toward us, swelling terrorist ranks.

This Election Day, we face a perverse twist on what political professionals call "the mommy problem." You might remember this from *The West Wing*.

Flying back to Paris after writing most of this, I happened upon the seventh season of Aaron Sorkin's White House fantasy. Jimmy Smits plays an Obamaesque candidate opposing Alan Alda, a reasonable Republican. In the script, as in reality today, Americans feel threatened by crises and want a firm hand.

"When voters want a national daddy, someone tough and strong, they vote Republican," Smits' campaign manager explains. "When they want a mommy to give them jobs, health care policy, the equivalent of matzo-ball soup, they vote Democratic."

So who's our daddy? If the option is Donald Trump, I'd prefer to be an orphan. Give me Hillary Clinton in a pantsuit anytime. Please take the time to ponder what is at risk. We will not have a second chance.

Our Trojan Horse's Ass

DECEMBER 4, 2016, PARIS – Tonight at bedtime, reflect on the scariest tragicomedies since Antiquity and then eat a large sausage pizza before falling asleep. Your worst nightmare, I humbly submit, won't approach the reality our world now faces.

If this sounds like demented raving, do your own analysis. Look at classic cases of megalomania over three millennia. Consider what Donald Trump is already doing, and who is helping him do it. If you're not terrified, you've already dozed off.

A president-elect who communicates by one-way 140-character brain farts is assembling a cast of characters no one from Aeschylus to Orwell ever imagined. The dress circle and the cheap seats love it. The rest of us watch in stupefied silence.

Sensible people bang alarms loud enough to wake the dead. Temperatures and oceans inexorably rise. Desperate human tides besiege borders. Tyrants shrug off Geneva accords on civilized behavior. Greedheads plunder. And nothing happens.

Of course, the mess we are in accrued over time, and all presidents, including the lame-duck incumbent, bear varying degrees of blame. Now we need to make things better, not destroy them beyond any repair.

Trump is already throwing his working-class faithful to Wall Street wolves. He infuriated China and embraced the mass-murderer Philippine leader who called our sitting president a son of a whore. His secret octopus holdings remain intact.

Soon we may not even be able to watch. "Journalist" Sean Hannity, among others, wants Trump to ban real reporters from the White House. He claims "they" backed Hillary Clinton. Take a long look at Steve Bannon.

In 2009, I co-edited *Dispatches*, a quarterly that won praise but collapsed because each issue was prohibitively expensive: $25, the price of a crap bottle of Beaujolais at Sardi's. Our fifth and last issue, on the environment, was titled "Endgame."

"As legend goes," I wrote in the intro, "Paul Revere galloped all night from Boston to Lexington shouting, "The British are coming!" Men grabbed their muskets, and now Americans don't have to drink tea every day at 4."

Then I imagined a modern-day Revere ride: Television ignores it because, late and impromptu as it is, no one gets it on tape. Accounts of it flash around the Internet, some accurate, many skewed. Then the interactive crowd weighs in: The British are coming—what's your opinion? Talk show clowns impugn the motives of an insomniac silver-smith; cable news commentators hold forth (What does he mean by the British are coming?). Before long, Minutemen are too busy negotiating book contracts to worry about Redcoats.

"Profit would be part of it. Hey, I'd love to fight, but later. My shop just got a shipment of Union Jacks and portraits of King George."

That seems awfully quaint in retrospect. Today, Trump's dissemblers with unlimited resources and unbound by conscience define their own twisted "post-truth" reality like the porkers on Orwell's Farm that believe some animals are more equal than others.

No one who cares about what America is supposed to be can sit this one out. Three branches of government, a docile press, and over-enthusiastic law enforcement can in four years corrupt functioning democracy beyond repair.

China, unfettered by democratic niceties, is fast scooping up dwindling global resources. Russia is exploiting its Trump windfall, cementing Bashar al-Assad in place while Europe is destabilized with refugees. And so on.

Protests at home, without broad public support, only enforce the authoritarians' push toward tougher, meaner policing. Pissing and moaning on Facebook is futile if a critical mass cannot coalesce into action.

If we don't react when a president-elect suggests revoking citizenship for burning the flag, you know we are at the edge. Even the late hide-bound Antonin Scalia acknowledged that as protected speech under the First Amendment.

So what can we do?

—Above all, give a shit. This is for real, and if we cannot box the crazies headed toward the White House it will be permanent. Read, discuss, call, write, organize, demonstrate, boycott, prosecute, recall.

—Look beyond personal interest. Those 1,000 Carrier plant workers in Indiana are happy Trump saved their jobs. But there are 320 million of us. One-off giveaways undermine tax bases and set bad precedents. Those who benefit pay later.

—Pick your own cause. Far too much is at stake for anyone to weigh in against it all. Educators and parents can fight for better schools. Editors and reporters know what they have to do. It all matters.

—Support others' causes. Those guys freezing their asses off in Dakota focus light on a national scourge: big-oil encroachment backed by law enforcement. It's not about "native Americans." That defines Indians but also most of the rest of us.

—Study the Constitution, with its Bill of Rights and all amendments.

—Linger a while on the key words: "We, the people." We get the government we deserve. If it's corrupt, we're corrupt. If we don't fix it, that's our failing. Start thinking about 2018 and 2020.

—And take heart. With all her negatives, Hillary won the popular vote by 2.5 million ballots; another 7 million went to others. Trump, no neo-con, is just an ordinary conman seeking maximum adulation. If he senses ignominious failure, he can be moved.

This is not as hard as it might seem. Just reread Shakespeare and tape another picture of your kids to the refrigerator.

This Is a Coup d'Etat, Plain and Simple

JANUARY 14, 2017, TUCSON - Now it is clear: we are seeing a coup d'etat. And its perpetrators, aided by citizens' apathy and wishful thinking, don't even need to gas up tanks or muzzle the media. This is exactly how democracies die.

We can stop this and emerge stronger—but only if enough of us grasp what is at stake and take action. Put aside political leanings and polemics to spend a moment assessing for yourself what you see unfolding.

Here, for what it's worth, is the view of a reporter who has covered coups in sizeable republics, evil empires and banana backwaters for a very long time.

Donald Trump is our chief executive, a term-limit civil servant bound by laws and common values to serve us all. Congressmen represent entire constituencies, not just partisans within them. Justices swear to be fair-minded and impartial.

One day after a departing president showed us our best side, outlining historic growth after crippling decline and pleading for unity in magnanimous terms that moved many to tears, his successor showed us our worst.

Though trounced by popular vote, Trump acts as if we handed him a crown. That storybook emperor skulked off when a kid pointed out he was naked. Trump simply flips us the finger and commits one indecent act after another.

Even if, against all economic odds , he could cut deals that made Americans richer at the expense of others, is that all matters? Consider the consequences in a volatile world bristling with arms and facing climatic endgame.

Trump's siding with Vladimir Putin rather than our incumbent leader falls between treachery and treason. It defines a man who puts his own ego above all else. With dazzling hypocrisy, his party criticizes him yet takes little action.

Republicans' disregard for propriety—trying to abolish ethics oversight as they steamroll approval of top officials tainted by vested interests, nepotism and crackpot extremism—reveals contempt for a citizenry they presume is stupid.

Already, a mad scramble is on to strip protection from natural splendor that took eons to evolve, sacred Indian sites, endangered aquifers and virgin wilderness for immediate plunder by a rapacious few with no regard for generations to come.

Our failsafe, beyond the three branches, is a permanent Fourth Estate: the press, now the "news media." For all the failings of its worst components, it is vital to us. Its best components set a global standard.

Trump's "press conference" swept away any lingering doubt of demagogic intention. He was an imperious, insulting bully who dismissed substance with inane generality, focusing not on domestic or world crises but on his own self-image.

When a reporter asked about his tax returns, he said the American people weren't interested. "I don't think they care at all," he sneered, thrusting a finger at his questioner. "I think you care."

Here is Trump in, well, a nutshell. A free society and its press are inseparable. Point one in our Bill of Rights. A dictator's first move is to discredit news media and replace them with big-lie propaganda, which is why *Breitbart* "News" had a front seat.

Presidential news conferences began as simple briefings: an executive answering to the people who hired him via the press. Now live TV allows leaders to play to the public, bypassing reporters who might pin them down with hard facts.

News executives let George W. Bush choreograph with pre-chosen questioners. Barack Obama imposed draconian means to plug leaks but answered questions when asked. Trump dismisses non-cheerleaders as unruly children.

Presidential news conferences began as simple briefings: an executive answering to the people who hired him via the press. Now live TV allows leaders to play to the public, bypassing reporters who might pin them down with hard facts.

CNN revealed an open secret, an unsubstantiated but solidly based report that Russians had taped Trump in a honey trap. Big whoop: a businessman who boasts of sexual prowess hired a prostitute. A simple denial would suffice.

But Trump went nuclear. "Fake news!" he thundered at a CNN reporter seeking clarity, cutting him off. Then a question came from Ian Pannell of BBC, a seasoned pro with the most credible, comprehensive global news purveyor I know.

"BBC," Trump said. "That's another beauty."

As for substance, Trump asserted: "(There are) 96 million really wanting a job and they can't get it. You know that story—the real number. That's the real number. So that's the way it is."

No, NPR noted in a running fact-check, the real number is 7.5 million. We are at full employment: 4.7 percent. More jobs would spike inflation. Trump included people not in the work force, including students, retirees and stay-at-home parents.

The man is a total fool—or he thinks that the rest of us are.

Meryl Streep brought this down to basic humanity at the Golden Globe Awards. More than a chief executive, she said, a president defines who we are. To illustrate, she chose an image many of us still can't get out of our heads.

Displeased by New York Times' reporter Serge Kovaleski, he mocked a condition that makes the man's bent right arm and hands move uncontrollably. Trump denies it, telling us to believe him rather than our own eyes.

Among so many outrages, some scare me to my core.

Trump approached truth, unintended, in one of his absurd tweets: "Is this Nazi Germany?" He was complaining that the CIA hovered over him. But his Big-Lie demagoguery evokes far too much of a Fiihrer elected by a fearful, hurting nation.

He is an equal-opportunity bigot, not specifically anti-Semitic. His free-form ill-informed extremism, mercurial with no clear worldview, risks eventual conflict with China and Russia. For now, there is the unholy land.

The man named as our ambassador to Israel has said that people like me are no better than Nazi guards who herded Jews to their death. That is, we Jews who believe that a separate Palestine is essential to Israel's survival and global stability.

My name and nose mark me as Jewish, but my religion is honest journalism, a belief that whoever or whatever created this world needs the help of reporters to keep it spinning as planned.

Since 1967, I've seen Holy Land hatreds grow in response to perceived injustice. We can't bomb those away. The terrorism Trump blames on Obama is rooted in our conduct of needless unwinnable war in Iraq.

But reporting loses all meaning if a society disregards fact and documented history. Without a grip on reality, we are lost. We need schools that prepare kids to see the world as it is. Yet Trump gives us Betsy DeVos.

An elitist billionaire, DeVos pushes private charter schools that earn profits while educating a chosen few and condemning others to black-board jungles that turn out barely literate masses to work cheap and believe what they're told.

Finland, in contrast, has the world's best schools because all of them are public. If rich people want their kids properly educated, they have to raise the level for everyone.

There is so much more; a cabinet of wolves to watch over us sheep; the sham of keeping Trump family business separate from ours; the ignominious rush to disrupt Obamacare for no reason but scorn for the man whose name it bears.

That last is the kicker. The Affordable Health Care is flawed because Congress rejected a single-payer approach so big business could profit. Republicans are repealing it before they know what might eventually take its place.

Politicians who insist that the life of unformed fetuses is sacred are prepared to let people die before their time before they can't afford our absurdly high medical costs.

So what to do?

First, think of cockroaches infesting a dark room. When you flip on the light, they scurry for the baseboards. If not, a can of Raid does the trick. That's Congress. Each voter only has to focus on two senators and a representative.

Even in gerrymandered states, voter turnout is low; committed opposition can defeat anyone. Call, write, sign petitions, attend town halls, organize protests and get to know aides who listen to reason. Be polite, persuasive—and persistent.

For a useful plan, go to www.indivisible.org, a report by former congressional staff workers. It began by focusing on how Tea Party amateurs inveigled their way onto Capitol Hill, it now focuses on 2020.

For a sense of how the cockroach kings put their narrow interests over ours, take a close look at Mitch McConnell, whose latest outrage was to stonewall a moderate Supreme Court nominee for nearly a year. If Trump proposes a partisan justice, compel Congress to stonewall another four years.

Our would-be emperor needs constant watching. More than anything else, he craves adulation. Boycott his brand. Remind his enthusiasts of every broken promise. If he senses the nation's mood harden against him, he will likely respond.

Coup leaders habitually entrench themselves with firepower and mass arrests. They tear up existing laws to write their own. Ours depend only on our apathy and ignorance. If we can't stop them cold, we deserve whatever befalls us.

II. "IT CAN'T HAPPEN HERE"? LOOK AROUND

In the Strangest Country on Earth

AUGUST 03, 2020, ORO VALLEY, ARIZONA - It is lunacy to open schools too early, the Fruit Lady told me, and after driving a school bus for 41 years she ought to know. "Those kids are all arms and mouths," she said. "Tell them anything, and their first word is, 'Why?'"

"You think they'll keep safe distances?" she asked. It wasn't a question. "Little ones are all over each other. They hug you, sneeze on you. Middle-school kids are the worst, spoiled by busy parents. How do you protect teachers, staff—or bus drivers?"

The Fruit Lady is the sort of voter Democrats need in purple states like Arizona. She is 69, retired and divorced after 45 years when her husband got fed up with peaches. With part-time hired help, her pick-'em-yourself orchard hasn't made money in two years.

Rising prices eat into her pension and social security checks. Tax cuts for the rich paid for more fancy houses along the highway north of Tucson but did not trickle down to her hardscrabble acre or the clapped-out ex-mobile homes on rutted roads behind them.

And now a killer plague stalks the state, getting steadily worse despite nonsensical happy talk from a president who allowed it to run wild yet demands that schools and businesses get going again. She sticks close to home with her trees and tomato vines.

After we talked for a while, the Fruit Lady sniffed out a likely liberal.

"I should tell you," she said, "I'm for Trump."

I left Tucson in 1967 for a life as a foreign correspondent, eager to probe all those corrupt dysfunctional societies I'd read about. After poking into the depths on six continents, I have found the strangest of them all right here where I started out.

The Fruit Lady has a name, and her quotes should be attributed.
When I first reported around here as a student, we even added street
addresses. It is a different America now. First Amendment aside,
people worry about what they say in public.

Polls and pundits mislead. That hoary "silent majority" is all over the
place. Facts are what anyone thinks they are. Labels replace nuanced
analysis. A wannabe despot condones wholesale death to get reelected.
His cultists find someone else to blame.

Trump people with bedsheet-sized flags and bumper stickers are easy
to spot but hard to interview. They know they're right. Period. But
the kindly Fruit Lady likes to talk. I battled wasps for a basket of ripe
peaches and then sat down with her.

"Oh, I know he is arrogant," she said, "but he says what he means,
and he's doing a good job." Joe Biden? "He's an idiot, and he has
dementia. My sister knows dementia, and he has it." I asked if she
had other sources.

"I listen to Fox sometimes," she said. She won't look at the *Arizona
Daily Star*, owned by a conservative chain. "It's a liberal rag." I asked
what she read instead. "Just the Bible." But is Trump a good Christian?
"The Lord works in mysterious ways."

A wannabe despot condones wholesale death to get reelected. His cultists find someone else to blame.

She wants the Wall, the higher the better. After 45 years in a place
Mexicans settled seven generations ago, making a desert bloom, she
learns from Trump they are rapists and murderers. "With me here
alone," she said, "I don't trust them on my property."

She denies climate change despite a freak lightning storm that ignited
dry pines and burned 120,000 acres of the nearby mountain. Heat rises
each year as endemic drought worsens. Scant rain falls at the wrong
time for crop cycles. She irrigates from a dwindling aquifer and doesn't

worry about it. In any case, Judgment Day is nigh.

"The world is coming to an end," she said. Devout Christians will go to heaven—you, too, she added, because Jesus was a Jew—but all those Muslims and Buddhists and whatnot will find that a 110-degree Tucson summer is chilly compared to what awaits them.

And Covid-19? "I turn off the news when they talk about it," she said. It's a plot by the godless Chinese that the Lord will sort out. "We should have nothing to do with them. Around here, when people see something made in China, they refuse to buy it."

But, I said, after the Chinese tried to hide it, they came clean on Jan. 9 and airlifted protective gear to America. Trump at first praised China's reaction. He called the virus a Democratic hoax until mid-March. She gave me that look: don't waste your breath.

"The China virus" is Trump's gospel, and Republican candidates play that to the hilt, no one more than Martha McSally, now fighting for her appointed Senate seat. Driving home, I passed the Safeway that now symbolizes how badly America has gone wrong.

In 2011, Rep. Gabrielle Giffords drew a crowd outside the Safeway for her usual "Congress on Your Corner" parlay with constituents. A drug-addled, rightwing misogynist opened fire with a 9mm pistol, killing six and wounding 20 more. Giffords barely survived a shot to the head.

McSally lost the Republican primary in a special election, and then the next general election, to replace Giffords. She succeeded in 2014, winning a House seat by 67 votes after five weeks of recounts. In 2018, she ran for the Senate, and Kyrsten Sinema beat her. But the governor later named her to fill John McCain's empty chair.

McSally opposes Mark Kelly, Gabby Gifford's popular astronaut husband against whom her "I-was-a-pilot" sounds lame. The Democrats say Mitch McConnell has put at least $20 million in PAC funds into her campaign, desperate to keep her shaky seat.

"China is to blame for this pandemic and the death of thousands of Americans," one McSally ad says, with a Bloomberg news clip saying the Chinese hid the early outbreak. A close look shows it is dated Jan. 4, five days before China shared genome sequences.

Then it got personal. An ad claimed Kelly invested hundreds of thousands of dollars in China. In fact, those were mutual funds, including Chinese securities, he had already sold. She, however, disclosed last August that her own funds held Chinese stocks, including Tencent, which invested in World View Enterprises. Which takes this deeper.

In 2012, World View's co-directors persuaded county supervisors to build a $15 million spaceport in Tucson for high-flying tourism. Kelly was hired to manage flight crews. New people now run the company, Kelly moved on, and the spaceport is still there. McSally's ad saying Kelly "ripped off taxpayers for $15 million" is an outrageous lie.

McSally, after criticizing Trump before he was elected, cheers his every move. She was the one who sneered at a polite question from Manu Raju of CNN. "You're a liberal hack," she said, "I'm not talking to you." Then she boasted about that on social media.

These mosaic pieces reveal a corrupted ill-informed nation in which truth matters less by the month. So far, political vitriol plays out largely in dueling yard signs. Still, the potential is frightening in a nation armed to the teeth.

As Covid-19 rages on and artificial Wall Street underpinnings erode toward collapse, it is likely a Biden administration will veer back toward sanity. But the place I left in the 1960s, the land of the free and the home of the brave, has changed beyond recognition.

Next door to the Fruit Lady, a sign on the lawn reflects a different extreme: "Any Functioning Adult—2020." I would have gone in to ask questions but another sign on the high chain link fence read in bold letters: "Beware of the dogs."

The Big Picture: Caveat Lector

JULY 14, 2020, LAKE POWELL, ARIZONA – The young guy at the helm wasn't thinking about a raging pandemic, a raving president, or anything else beyond submerged logs and sand bars as we flashed past spectacular rock formations on Lake Powell. That morning, his wife said she was leaving him.

Sparing him questions, I reflected instead on a conversation in Paris with a visiting editor pal as we watched flotsam drift down the Seine through the heart of a city that has seen so much during its 2,000 years.

Americans once saw news as a lake, he said. With a sense of its shape and depths, they shared a common idea of reality when the water suddenly got rough. News is now a river. People see only what floats by if they happen to be watching, with little thought to its origin or import.

If black type suddenly screams, "China Invades Taiwan," it is too late to react. Stories that matter are part of a continuing process that confounds headlines. Reporters on the ground, permanently in place with solid sources, need to watch closely as ripples build into waves.

We need newspapers. "Dead trees" is passé; they are also online. Reporters on the spot, with time to reflect and space to write at length, need to tell us why stories matter.

We need correspondents to warn us of smoldering conflicts ready to flare into flame and runaway pathogens leaders try to hide. We need local reporters to expose authorities who betray our trust and erode the underpinnings of democracy. But we're losing both.

Solid reporting competes for attention with infinite crap, from outright propaganda to well-intentioned karaoke journalism, off-key with garbled lyrics. Closed borders, official harassment and government cover-ups mask truth. Today's watchword is *caveat lector*. Reader beware.

Those who care about our overheated, overamped planet need to do what real journalists do: Question everything. Test one source against others. Tune out noise to listen for a ring of truth. Read history with an eye on the individuals who make it. Times change; human nature doesn't.

History doesn't just repeat itself. It gets more complex, with cumulative impact. Past mistakes, geophysical as well as geopolitical, have pushed us to the edge. Billions struggle for their very survival, and we are fast running out of time to mitigate, much less resolve, long-ignored crises.

Donald Trump, buoyed by American inattention, is the most dangerous man on Earth. He ignores past miscalculations at home and abroad to push greed-obsessed, shortsighted policies in calamitous new directions. Lake Powell is a brushstroke in an alarming global big picture.

The vast reservoir, 140 feet deep on average, is a monument to human folly. It flooded Glen Canyon during the 1970s, submerging dramatic sandstone gorges and rock wonders carved out over eons, inundating ancient remains of civilizations that knew how to coexist with nature.

Engineers dammed the Colorado River to harness its flow through the Grand Canyon. Along with Hoover Dam farther west, it ensured a steady water supply to Arizona and surrounding states and protected downstream banks after occasional freak heavy snowfall in the Rockies.

The reservoirs made deserts bloom, irrigating fields of alfalfa and cotton, orchards and sprawling cattle ranches. Copper mines and industries boomed. Fast-growing cities with lush green golf courses and exotic gardens squandered water as if there was no tomorrow.

Tomorrow is upon us. The water-starved West suffers endemic drought, rising heat, forest fires and steadily growing populations. Vast amounts are lost to evaporation. Magnificent splendor is gone forever. The "tamed" Colorado is a trickle as it enters Mexico and dies in salt marshes.

Across America, we need to cut back and reengineer. Trump does the opposite, letting mines, fossil-fuel producers and agrobusiness plunder at will. Slashing regulations, he says, makes America great. Abroad, his narrow focus raises the potential for conflict, cold or hot, to an unimaginable degree.

Yet with so much at stake, our tower-of-babble news media no longer shape a critical mass of public opinion. Without a clear idea of the existential threats we face, we cannot do much about them.

After a lifetime of "mainstream" reporting, it is time to step back and say what I see and hear, unfiltered, about an imperiled world as it is. My goal is to help readers connect the dots into big pictures.

Television once helped set the agenda, teaming with newspapers to add images and analysis to bring distant reality into living rooms at home. But take a look, for instance, at *CBS Morning News* on the network that gave us Murrow and Cronkite.

It begins with a montage, "Your World in 90 Seconds." The other day, that was a minute of Trump snippets and a video, suspiciously improbable, of a father trying to keep three infants from besieging an open refrigerator. Cute. But what about that world?

We need newspapers. "Dead trees" is passé; they are also online. Reporters on the spot, with time to reflect and space to write at length, need to tell us why stories matter. Without them, TV would be mostly conjecture and argument.

In the last decade, American newspapers have cut more than half their newsroom staffs, and that is it not nearly the worst of it. They are bought up, eviscerated or put to death. Hedge funds and private equity firms trade them as if they were pork-bellies or junk bonds.

I started out in 1964 at the *Arizona Daily Star*, one of two thriving family-owned Tucson dailies. Staff reporters, the *Associated Press* and other agencies filled news pages. An editorial board and the publisher wrote opinion. Advertisers had no say in what went into the paper. The line between us, unlike Trump's porous border wall, was impenetrable.

Most publishers back then believed in civic responsibility. Some were independent; others leaned right or left. But all knew their fortunes depended on credibility and public trust. Editors stormed out the door if ordered to slant news.

When John S. Knight took his *Akron Beacon Journal* public in 1960 to start the Knight-Ridder chain, he told financiers, "I do not intend to be your prisoner." He built an admirable empire and then died in 1981 before having to rethink his motto: Don't be afraid of change.

Knight-Ridder covered the world with intrepid pros from its star papers, including the *Philadelphia Inquirer, Miami Herald* and *Detroit Free Press*. In 2003, its Washington bureau was alone in reporting that Iraq no longer had the banned weapons George W. Bush claimed it did.

Los Angeles Times and *Chicago Tribune* correspondents were mostly superb, deep diggers with a poetic bent. Editors allowed them ample wordage and generous expenses. They often outshined the *New York Times* with stories that brought to life other cultures for readers back home.

The Tribune Company bought the *L.A. Times* in 2000 and ran it into the ground from Chicago. Real estate scavenger Sam Zell acquired the company to sell off pieces. When a reporter asked at a newsroom meeting about quality, he glared and told her: "Fuck you." Zell moved on, but the saga continued. In 2018, a billionaire doctor rescued the *Times*, a shadow of its former self.

Knight-Ridder, meantime, was swallowed up in 2006 by McClatchy, which choked on it. After eviscerating fine old papers, it filed for bankruptcy early this year. The California-based chain, owned by the same family for 163 years, will likely be run by Chatham Asset Management, the New Jersey hedge fund that controls the *National Enquirer.*

As America turned ironically inward after 9/11, and recession bit hard, the industry crumbled. Ads shifted to the internet, which provided news for free. Executives tried to slash their way to profitability, firing journalists and letting advertisers influence what they called "content."

Wall Street raiders scavenge "properties" with what is known as vulture capital, although even buzzards wait until their prey dies before moving in. The most voracious is Alden Capital Fund, with various subsidiaries all under SoftBank of Japan.

In 2018, Alden swooped in on the *Denver Post,* and its staff rebelled. Its CEO brushed off appeals to maintain its quality or find a buyer that would. Alden issues edicts and fires those who don't comply. In a business built on asking questions, it routinely says nothing.

"The public shaming of Alden for its greed and disregard for newspapers' historic community-serving missions hasn't seemed to make an iota of difference in the company's behavior," media analyst Ken Doctor wrote in the *Nieman Report* in 2018.

Alden could reinvest its 17 percent profit margin in the newsrooms, he said, or put its properties actively on the market. It hasn't. Its books are as opaque as Trump's taxes, but a lawsuit and sources suggest it uses newspaper profits for real estate deals and risky ventures.

The *New York Times* just ran a long frontpage profile of one Alden victim, the *Mercury* in Pottstown, Pennsylvania, a scrappy little daily with 30 journalists that displayed two Pulitzers at its 25,000-square-foot landmark building, now sold off to be a boutique hotel.

The *Mercury,* with a daily circulation of 27,500 across three counties, is down to a single diehard reporter: Evan Brandt, 55 with a wife and kids, who makes $47,000 a year and works from his third-story attic.

When Alden took over, he drove to the CEO's lavish Long Island home with a sign reading, "Invest in Us or Sell us." He was ejected from the property without a hearing, and the hedge fund has done neither.

Now Alden is after the *Chicago Tribune*. Early in July, it negotiated a deal for a third of its stock now, and it appears ready to push for a takeover in 2021.

Alden's style cost it the grand prize. Gannett has been the big dog since it moved out of upstate New York, subsuming hundreds of dailies under its flagship, *USA Today*. Last year, it rejected an Alden offer and merged with *GateHouse Media*, keeping the Gannett name.

Now the vultures are circling my old Tucson paper. The afternoon *Citizen* is a memory. Gannett bought it in 1976. but killed it in 2009 to profit from its assets when circulation dropped to 17,000 from its 1960s peak of 60,000. But the *Star* survives. So far.

The Pulitzers bought the *Star* in the 1970s, long after the family's *St. Louis Post-Dispatch* lost its luster. In 2005, Lee Enterprises of Davenport, Iowa, added Arizona to its galaxy: along with the Star, it owns the *Sun* in Flagstaff, down the road from Lake Powell.

Lee stripped the *Star* bare, with an overworked and underpaid small staff. Its editorial page is mostly unpaid op-ed contributions and a few syndicated columns. Now Lee Enterprises is on the skids. Alden has taken a small of bite of it and seems hungry for more.

Public funding and philanthropy help fill the widening void, particularly for investigations into single-topic stories. But 18,000 communities have no local news coverage. And few newspapers give readers a cogent overview of interlinked global crises.

Technology is not the answer. Covering city councils and school boards by remote cameras is no better than stenography. What matters happens in the hallways. World news pooled from shared networks of untested stringers only scratches at the surface.

The spiral downward now heads toward freefall. Americans badly need reporting on a runaway pandemic, but newspaper cutbacks limit their ability to provide it. Advertising wanes and hard-pressed families cancel subscriptions.

A Pew study late last year found nearly half of Americans rely on Facebook for news, essentially exchanging dubious information with their friends. Television follows closely behind. Only 18 percent still read print newspapers.

But television stations, with few reporters of their own, are increasingly politicized. Sinclair Broadcasting is a rightwing behemoth that champions Trump. It owns 193 stations, reaching 40 percent of America. If FCC negotiations are successful, that could expand to 72 percent.

Sinclair distributes canned "must run" segments, neither fair nor balanced, to all of its stations. Meantime, online organizations like *Breitbart News* follow the tactical approach that Steve Bannon once outlined simply: "Flood the zone with shit."

Tragically, few Americans seem to care about all of this. Trump's relentless "fake news" assaults and mindless generalities about "the media" shake faith in the best of American organizations. And it is hard to exaggerate the danger.

Consider that distraught young helmsman on Lake Powell. His mind is on a wife who is packing her bags and a bunch of other worries. But if he doesn't keep an eye on those submerged logs and sandbars, and he goes down with his boat, nothing else will matter.

Saint Donald and the Dragon

JUNE 25, 2020, TUCSON, ARIZONA — Whether Donald Trump slips into history as a bitter laugh line, or he weasels his way into a second term, his ham-handed hubris toward China has done more to change the shape of global geopolitics since the rise and fall of Adolf Hitler's Third Reich.

Trump lost face in China by alternately bullying and fawning over Xi Jinping in full public view. That turned an essential ally in confronting global crises into a wary hostile adversary bent on muscling aside the United States for world supremacy.

Previous American policy, engagement, was a discreet minuet. Both partners took intricate steps at arm's length. Trump's approach was estrangement. He berated China in public for dirty dealing, declared a trade war. Yet when it suited his needs, he shifted to abject flattery.

As Trump charges, China steals intellectual property, knocks off American products and infringes on copyrights. But his tariffs and taunts reversed decades of progress toward common accord. Now scapegoating China for his failure to contain Covid-19 provokes unmarked anger.

Trump repeats a one-word sneer, "'Gina," and talks of "kung flu." Republicans follow his lead. In a crucial race in Arizona, Sen. Martha McSally's ads berate "those communists." She says her favored opponent has "Chinese investments." So do most Americans with mutual funds.

Republicans slur Joe Biden as being close to China. Democrats explain why a lifelong statesman steeped in history knows better than to jab sticks at a dragon that is waking from a long sleep, eating our lunch and getting hungry again an hour later.

China is fortifying its nuclear arsenal and deep-water fleet. It patrols vital sea lanes in the South China Sea, plants its flag from the ocean floor to the dark side of the moon and bribes its way into poor states across the world for strategic materials, markets and U.N. votes.

Badly in need of the West, China is open to quiet diplomacy if both sides can claim victory. But Xi, leader for life in a society that thinks in millennia rather than four-year terms, is in no hurry. The Middle Kingdom can endure setbacks and lasting pain in pursuit of global domination.

The past matters in China, which suffered a century of humiliation under European and Japanese occupation after so many successive emperors kept foreign barbarians at bay. When Japan was finally driven out in 1945, two opposing factions fought for control.

America spent heavily to pick up the pieces of World War II. It helped forge a United Nations and championed democracy in a postwar world. But it backed the wrong side in China. Mao Zedong took a sharp left turn and slammed the door.

The world knew little of the famine that took at least 30 million lives—perhaps up to 55 million—in the early 1960s. Reuters was later allowed in briefly, but Red Guards expelled its correspondent in 1969 after holding him captive for 777 days. At one point, they tortured his cat to death in front of him.

Reporters saw China through the looking glass from Hong Kong, interviewing diplomats and travelers to amplify guesswork about who stood where in ceremonial photos.

Early in 1971, I bumped into F. Tillman Durdin, a dour *New York Times'* Asian hand who didn't smile much. He grinned like a Cheshire cat as he fluttered a telegram at me as if it announced he had won the Irish Sweepstakes. It was better. "This," he said, "is my China visa."

After a hint from Peking, Henry Kissinger flew secretly to Peking. Richard Nixon followed with reporters in tow. James Reston's analysis in the *Times* is still fresh today: "China's attitude and tactics toward the United States are obviously changing, but her strategy and principles remain the same."

Trump missed that message. John Bolton's new book says he pleaded with Xi to help him win a second term, offering favorable trade terms in exchange. He praised ethnic cleansing and brutal concentration camps for a million Muslims in Xinjiang.

Xi concluded the obvious. American moralizing about democratic principles, press freedom and the rest is cynical hypocrisy. Trump—malleable, self-obsessed and ignorant of global realities—is far more paper than tiger.

But Xi, leader for life in a society that thinks in millennia rather than four-year terms, is no hurry. The Middle Kingdom can endure setbacks and lasting pain in pursuit of global domination.

Young Americans now face the prospect of a Chinese-accented world in which governments can be blatantly corrupt, free expression is muzzled, and individuals are punished for resisting the party line. China wants resources and subservience. Human rights are not part of the picture.

Bob Dylan, reflecting on generational change in a *New York Times'* interview, observed: "We have a tendency to live in the past, but that's only us. Youngsters... have no past, so all they know is what they see and hear, and they'll believe anything... That's going to be the reality." Our schools should be teaching Mandarin.

Few young people grasp China's sense of manifest destiny. Armed conflict, if unlikely, is a grim prospect. A nuclear exchange would devastate both sides. Assault by sea is iffy. A few Covid-19 cases put a U.S. aircraft carrier out of service. Wars are won or lost on the ground.

In the Korean War, which broke out 70 years ago on June 25, 120,000 Chinese troops overran U.S. Marines and soldiers. By the armistice in 1953, China had deployed nearly 3 million men.

"Ripley's Believe It or Not!" once noted an old calculation when China had 600 million inhabitants. If they marched four abreast at military pace, they would never stop coming. Newborns would grow up and join the ranks. China's population is now 1.4 billion.

Mao's old People's Liberation Army is two-million strong, the world's largest, nearly twice the total of American armed forces. And it is aggressively on the move.

Chinese and Indian troops clashed on June 15 along the disputed Himalayan frontier, where India is building a north-south road for trade between the world's two most populous nations. In a tense new atmosphere, each side has amassed thousands of troops.

Chinese soldiers with nail-studded clubs and rocks killed at least 20 Indians, wounding many more. Beijing said little about the skirmish but admitted that a senior commander died. Any escalation would likely involve tanks and heavy artillery.

Narendra Modi last year imposed tight controls in Kashmir, pushing against Pakistani positions. Emboldened by a $3.5 billion U.S. arms deal and Trump's warm embrace, he is raising the heat. China backs Pakistan, where it is planning a naval base. India's fury at China for the June attack compounds simmering enmity against Pakistan. Each of the old foes has nukes; a showdown would risk involving the United States and China.

In the South China Sea, U.S. warships challenge Xi's right to restrict traffic to Asia and the Pacific. Near collisions have almost sparked hostilities. Diplomacy has protected Taiwan's independence since 1949. But Xi abruptly took over Hong Kong despite China's pledge to keep it autonomous until 2047. Today, anything can happen.

As Trump cuts aid to African countries, China moves in fast. Its ships are back again on the East African coast, which a Chinese fleet briefly colonized 500 years ago. A French Foreign Legion outpost was alone in the sleepy port of Djibouti until 9/11 when Americans built Camp Lemonnier as an African foothold. Now a PLA naval base effectively controls entry to the port.

Economic setbacks have delayed Xi's multi-trillion-dollar Belt and Road Initiative involving 70 countries, but a new trade route retraces Marco Polo's steps back to Italy. The old Silk Road links China to the Middle East and Asia Minor. For the rest, China can wait.

China tried to hide the coronavirus outbreak, but U.S. intelligence warned of it in December. By mid-January, courageous Chinese doctors, defying orders, spread the word. Correspondents converged on Wuhan for detailed accounts of the mysterious pathogen. The WHO and other governments worked urgently to contain it. World markets were shaken.

This was hardly a time to return to the 1960s with American reporters peering through opaque windows while Chinese state media show its own self-portrait to the world. Xi seized the moment.

After a March op-ed headline in the *Wall Street Journal* called China the sick weak man of Asia, China expelled the paper's three reporters. When Mike Pompeo responded harshly, China added the *New York Times, Washington Post* and others. Real dictators are better at tit-for-tat than aspiring ones.

In January and February, wrapping up a trade deal, Trump praised China's transparency and effective action in curbing the virus. In March, when it ran wild in America because of Trump's own inaction, he laid blame squarely on China and the WHO. Hanger-on Republicans ignored indisputable facts to echo his distortions.

Xi joined world leaders to confront the pandemic. He gave $2 billion to WHO, four times the annual dues that Trump withheld. World leaders see plainly who is at fault. The European Union now bans visitors from the United States. Chinese are welcome with open arms.

By turning his back on the world, Trump leaves it wide open to China. And as an ancient Middle Kingdom epigram puts it, a careful foot can step anywhere.

On Redacting a Wide, Wondrous World

MAY 26, 2020, TUCSON – A whiff of spice can take me back to a sundown in Sana'a, sprawled on carpet cushions, chewing khat with zonked-out Yemeni pals under bright stars atop a six-story skyscraper made of mud. A haunting chorus of muezzins wailed their call to prayer as they had for a thousand years.

We ate fahsi served on ornate brass platters: lamb cutlets stewed with chickpeas in cardamom, coriander and cumin (that is just the c's), laced with fiery pili-pili. Honey-pistachio pastries came with cups of green coffee I won't attempt to describe.

I left Tucson in the 1960s to roam the world in pursuit of news but also on a quest to find tucked-away treasures — to watch, listen, breathe in aromas and linger late at night to learn how the other 95 percent lived. Far and away, Sana'a was the jackpot.

That magical city, which legend dates back to Noah's son Shem, nestled in a valley 7,500-feet-high, among dramatic peaks. Narrow lanes dotted with donkey plop wound among the carved doorways, stained glass and alabaster façades of high-rise mud mansions. From above, it was an Arabian Nights fantasy in gingerbread.

In a warren of souks, alive with noise and color, we talked politics over hubble-bubble pipes. North Yemen was open to all comers. China built roads; Taiwan looked after F5 jets from America. North Korea did the stadiums; South Korea did the sewers. South Yemen was a Soviet vassal, but Moscow also sent financial and military aid up north.

Today, Sana'a is largely rubble, partly because of Raytheon Corporation bombs built in Tucson. Yemen, now unified but at war with itself, is the world's worst humanitarian disaster. Half of its 30 million people are starving, and Covid-19 spreads. Perhaps 200,000 combatants and civilians have been killed, perhaps many more. No one knows.

I am partial to old mud walls and tile, lost long ago to Tucson when developers tore out its old Mexican heart. But so much else in the world has been destroyed or closed off by conflict. Today, a world map with no-go areas inked over would look like the Mueller report redacted by William Barr.

As Yemen makes dead clear, Donald Trump's foreign policy is wreaking new levels of irreparable havoc in an interconnected world. And it exposes his single-minded pursuit of profit and his own personal interests.

Saudi Arabia waded into the civil war in 2015 with relentless airstrikes in the north on rebelling Shiites—Houthis. The kingdom blockaded food and medical supplies in what human rights observers call a deliberate, indiscriminate siege campaign.

Barack Obama authorized logistical support to counter Houthi shelling into Saudi Arabia, but he began to scale back as civilian casualties increased. Trump, in contrast, doubled down. Jared Kushner courted

Crown Prince Mohammed Bin Salman and worked out a 10-year arms sales package approaching a half trillion dollars.

Fury mounted in 2018 when the prince's goons lured Jamal Khashoggi to the Saudi consulate in Istanbul. They silenced his critical columns in *The Washington Post* by dismembering him with a bone saw. Trump shrugged that off with a few token words.

Sen. Mike Lee, a Utah Republican, joined Bernie Sanders in a bill to block arms sales to Saudi Arabia, invoking the War Powers Resolution to keep the American military out of foreign conflicts.

"We have been providing the bombs that the Saudi-led coalition is using, we have been refueling their planes before they drop those bombs, and we have been assisting with intelligence," Sanders said. "In too many cases our weapons are being used to kill civilians." In August, he noted, an American-made bomb hit a school bus, killing dozens of young boys and wounding many more.

The bill passed early in 2019, 54-46, but not enough senators could override Trump's veto. A *New York Times* investigation recently revealed the damning details.

Trump inherited crises that required defusing tension, strengthening European alliances and finding common ground with adversaries. The Middle East, especially, needed evenhanded diplomacy. His approach was the exact opposite.

In May 2017, Lee put Saudi arms sales on hold in the Armed Services Committee. Raytheon countered with its chief lobbyist: Mark Esper, now secretary of defense. Peter Navarro, the trade adviser, wrote a memo titled, "Trump Mideast arms sales deal in extreme jeopardy, job losses imminent." Sales soon resumed.

On the *Fox* business channel, Trump laid out his approach: "I want Boeing and I want Lockheed and I want Raytheon to take those orders and to hire lots of people to make that incredible equipment."

Day after day, Americans watch their president intone dire threats with jutting jaw and glowering brow, a striking echo of Mussolini. At home, his self-serving policies are plain to see. But few realize how much destruction and suffering he causes abroad.

Nothing in foreign policy can be seen in isolation. In America, "breaking news" deals with the moment. But human memories are long, and the past matters. NATO and the UN need cooperation to stifle conflict; Trump doesn't do cooperation. America First equates to America Only.

Trump inherited crises that required defusing tension, strengthening European alliances and finding common ground with adversaries. The Middle East, especially, needed evenhanded diplomacy. His approach was the exact opposite.

In his view, the massive assault on the Islamic State's caliphate was the end of terrorism, an American victory to bedazzle his base. In fact, Iraqis and Kurds did most of the in-close dying, and American non-policy creates far more terrorists than it suppresses.

Until Desert Storm took back Kuwait in 1990, Middle East geopolitics amounted to backgammon, with subtle moves and shifting strategies. George H. W. Bush chose not to push on to Baghdad, mindful of a power vacuum after Saddam Hussein.

But the Gulf War infuriated Osama bin Laden, who said a half million infidel U.S. troops, females included, on bases in Saudi Arabia defiled Islam's holiest sites. He formed Al Qaeda, which first attacked U.S. embassies in Africa.

After 9/11, George W. Bush pursued him in Afghanistan, then decided to finish off Saddam. That blasted the backgammon board all to hell. American torture embittered Sunnis, who created ISIS. When their caliphate was overrun, many fled to West Africa, linking up with other Islamic zealots who fled south when Libya fell.

Like pungent spices evoke Yemen, clunking wooden bells take me back to Timbuktu, knees gripping a camel hump with blue-turbaned Tuaregs headed into the dunes. That fabled center of Islamic learning on the Niger River dwarfed anything I had imagined.

I'd visit markets ablaze in color and then leave my shoes by carved wood doorways for tea with hospitable imams. Back at the French-run Sofitel, I'd swim while tourists sunbathed in bikinis. Dinner came with red wine unfazed by a journey from Burgundy.

Today, a wide stretch of West Africa is redacted off the map. Even armed convoys are wary of Timbuktu. Terrorists from Libya joined rebelling Tuaregs to occupy the city. Islamist fundamentalists destroyed much of it. French forces drove them out, but France has lost 41 men in Mali since 2013. Another 200 U.N. peacekeepers were killed.

Trump, uninterested in places with nothing to offer, wants to cut aid and U.S. military presence in Africa, where climate change he refuses to confront already forces millions to flee their homes.

Stepping back, the global order is changing. Trump's version of the pandemic—it is all China's fault—provokes scorn abroad. He mocked it for months as another Democratic hoax. Until mid-March, he praised Xi Jinping's openness and prompt action.

China hid the threat briefly until courageous doctors sounded alarms. By mid-January, the Chinese published vital data about the deadly coronavirus, but Trump ignored his experts' briefings. Had Obama left "a mess" (he didn't), that was three years ago.

With grim irony as Covid-19 spreads in America, Trump supporters who want to keep out foreigners are, at least for now, themselves turned away at borders.

Trump refused WHO tests that contained the virus elsewhere. He withheld funding and shunned a video summit to plot a common strategy. Xi stepped in with a $2 billion grant, equal to four years of America's dues.

Xi seized the moment to assert China's growing global role. For starters, Beijing would end Hong Kong's autonomy far sooner than agreed in the 1997 handover with Britain that pledged "one country, two systems" until 2047.

China contained Covid-19 with drastic surveillance, message control and lockdowns that are anathema to any free society. Trump is doing his part, inspiring dictators to muzzle their media with two words: fake news. He applauds Narendra Modi as he veers the world's biggest democracy toward Hindu hegemony.

After Trump saw he could not wish away the virus, he focused on twisting truth to elude blame. Meantime, crises deepen all over the map. Israel and Palestine face showdown. Kim Jong-un is building a bigger bomb. And all the rest.

Keeping the peace in today's world is no job for a greed-obsessed, clueless amateur, backed by private interests and corporations, each with their own to-do lists. A new president can fix some damage. But no one can bring back that sunset in Sana'a.

On Young Dogs and Old Tricks

MAY 20, 2020, TUCSON – I used to say the only difference between 23 and dead is all in the mind. Now, a lot closer to the latter than the former, not so much. But today age looms large in an America facing its most crucial elections ever.

A recent *Atlantic* headline asked, "Why Do Such Elderly People Run America?" Good question. Lots of young people with fresh ideas and new skills see their options in November—two men, 150 years old between them—as total wastes of space.

But the writer, 38, lost me fast. He called Donald Trump, Joe Biden and Bernie Sanders "three candidates divided by ideology but united in dotage." Dotage? Webster defines that as "senile decay marked by decline of mental poise and alertness." Fuck off, punk.

Ageism is a small-bore bias. Mostly, it reflects callow, shallow thinkers who generalize in data-clump shortcuts like their computers (which, BTW, their elders invented). Some people are couchbound rutabagas by 50; others remain brilliant into their 90s.

America now needs a seasoned statesman to restore decency at home and to steer it off the rocks abroad…As he turns the United States inward, China threatens to set a frightening new global standard for human values, freedoms and political philosophy.

For the CEO of an imperiled "free world," being old has value, even if he, or she, says "malarkey" for "bullshit." Founding Fathers fixed the minimum age for president at 35 back when male life expectancy was near 38. They wanted the oldest bulls in the herd.

A long life reveals over time how confronting the present requires an understanding of the past. Diplomacy demands an acquired feel for reading faces and anticipating how action might trigger reaction. Situations vary; human nature remains constant.

Age isn't Trump's problem. He has been a self-obsessed lying cheat since childhood. Biden may not fire up audiences that expect entertaining bombast, but he excels at what matters now: calmly finding common ground at home and abroad.

At 73, Trump dismisses his 77-year-old rival as "Sleepy Joe," too addled to speak without gaffes. I can't wait for pointed debate questions on climate and foreign policy. Perhaps Trump will take up Biden's challenge to a pushup contest.

Every president needs two crucial qualities: an ability to inspire the nation and a firm grip on real-world realities.

JFK swept into office at 43 with that brief, stirring Inaugural speech. "Ask not what your country can do for you—ask what you can do for your country." But he bumbled into war that devastated Vietnam, then Cambodia, rejecting Charles de Gaulle's warnings about what France had learned to its grief.

Obama, at 47, aced inspiration. He steered George W. Bush's trashed economy into a boom for which Trump claims credit. He was a leader on climate change and the deal to lower the heat in Iran. But Syrians ignored his line in the sand, Saudis pounded Yemen and Afghans kept on killing each other.

America now needs a seasoned statesman to not only restore decency at home but also steer it off the rocks abroad. Trump thwarts cooperation to contain a pandemic that is reshaping life on Earth. As he turns the United States inward, China threatens to set a frightening new global standard for human values, freedoms and political philosophy.

My own septuagenarian view is suspect. Consider instead wisdom that has held up for 2,000 years, Plutarch's essay titled, "Should an Old Man Engage in Politics?" A short summary: Of course, he should. Why burn down a living library?

Books about piloting a ship don't produce captains, he wrote, "unless those captains have often stood upon the stern to observe the struggles against wave and wind and stormy night." Leaders don't need physical strength; that is only necessary for the officers and troops at their command.

He added: "To take on menial and common work after practicing politics is like stripping away the dress of a free... woman, replacing it with an apron, and then forcing her to work in a tavern." We need fresh young comers like Alexandria Ocasio-Cortez for the future. Should she go back to mixing drinks in a Bronx bar when she gets old?

Judgment, frankness and wisdom develop slowly over time, Plutarch concluded, "so it makes no sense... that they no longer be of service."

For some, history begins when they decide to take notice. A student once told me the Vietnam War didn't matter; it was over before he was born. Alexander the Great was a bit before my time, I replied, but I knew he conquered much of the known world before he was old enough to buy cigarettes today in Arizona.

Alexander learned in war what Machiavelli wrote about political science 1,500 years later. Authoritarians gain power by playing dirty and keep it by making good on their threats, cowing their own people and their adversaries into submission.

America made itself great with a reverse tack, based on human nature's better angels. Leaders should be respected, if not loved, more than feared. Three branches would check and balance one another. The first item of the Bill of Rights enshrined a free press.

During the Reagan '80s, conservatives began to entrench oligarchy. They pushed public schools to discourage critical thinking and social sciences, creating a workaday class that enabled an elite to get increasingly rich. Bread and circuses worked for the Romans.

In 2016, with the internet and *Fox News*, they succeeded beyond their wildest dreams. But the unhinged narcissist who Republicans expected to manipulate has let a plague run amok, killing more than 100,000 and plunging America into depression. His cultists and hangers-on, unfazed, blame China, Obama and yet another Democratic hoax.

Young people must endure whatever comes next. At the rate we're going, scientists say, by 2070 much of our planet will be too hot and dry to support humans. Marine life is dying fast. Meantime, we face worsening plagues and endemic global conflict.

And yet those from 18 to 24 are the least likely to vote. Many dismiss Biden as a doddering old man, and they squander a ballot on a third-party candidate.

Last time, 12 percent of Bernie diehards voted for Trump, an outsider who would "drain the swamp." He brought in nastier alligators, along with water moccasins and leeches. Hillary Clinton won by three million ballots, but the Electoral College outcome turned on three states decided by fewer voters than can fill a decent-sized stadium.

Democrats can tax the über-rich and adopt health care if they win the White House and Congress. They can bring the federal deficit and the national debt back down from the stratosphere. But November is now or never.

Even if Trump squeaks by on a technicality decided in the packed Supreme Court, the oligarchy will entrench itself. Wilderness and national splendor will be lost forever at a galloping pace. Scientists expect polluted air and water, over time, to kill far more Americans than pandemics.

Biden, in my own opinion, can restore sanity at home and respect abroad. A quick-study vice president with a solid worldview can then take over in 2024 to rally a different kind of Congress toward serious reform.

This is hardly *Dancing With the Stars*. It is not about single issues, emotional appeal or decisions made in an earlier time. The stakes are our very survival.

The *Atlantic* piece began with that Super Tuesday incident Biden detractors cite to show he is too old. In his victory speech, he "mistook his wife for his sister." No, he didn't. The women had switched places behind him. He was momentarily surprised when he turned to introduce them.

It ends, as it should, with climate change, saying America needs "ideas and input from the generation...most affected by it." Of course. But altering the global ecosystem, like containing pandemics, is far beyond any one nation's possibilities.

Fresh young leaders must reverse climatic chaos. But first, an American president already trusted across the world can unite large nations that pollute and small ones that suffer from it. His age is irrelevant.

The World According to Trump

MAY 07, 2020, TUCSON – My favorite front page in a hometown paper splashes big letters across the top about a mysterious prowler. A small headline below says, "Two Dacron Women Feared Missing in Volcanic Disaster," with a tiny subhead: "Japan Destroyed." An arrow on a Pacific Ocean map is labeled, "Where Japan was formerly located."

The *National Lampoon's* Dacron Republic-Democrat in 1978 spoofed an obsession for "the local angle." Today, I wouldn't be surprised at something similar, for real, on my doorstep. America has never been so closely, and dangerously, focused on itself.

Transfixed by Donald Trump's depredations at home, few Americans reflect on the world of pain his self-focused folly causes abroad: conflicts flare, poverty deepens, terrorism thrives, human rights vanish, trade wars cripple the global economy.

He shuns cooperation, not only to contain a highly contagious new virus likely to kill millions but also to mitigate climate collapse and sea change that are pushing humanity toward a die-off of billions.

Depending on Trump's purpose, Xi Jinping is a brilliant transparent leader or a shameless cheat who hides evidence of a plague while robbing America blind. As a result, a wary China focuses on muscling aside America as world leader, one way or another.

Solid reporting abounds. The *Washington Post* won a Pulitzer for a series on how fast Earth is overheating. The *New York Times'* prize package exposed Russia's shadow wars—bombings, murder, bribes, disinformation—in Europe, the Middle East and Africa.

Yet a survey during Covid-19 isolation showed a slight increase in news readership while gaming and old TV reruns were off the charts. With so many choices for have-it-your-way news, people shape personal worldviews around their own prejudices.

In April, Fintan O'Toole of the *Irish Times* stunned Americans with an unsparing account of how their country appears from the outside. He wrote: "Over more than two centuries the United States has stirred a very wide range of feelings in the rest of the world: love and hatred, fear and hope, envy and contempt, awe and anger. But there is one emotion that has never been directed toward the US until now: pity.

"However bad things are for most other rich democracies, it is hard not to feel sorry for Americans. Most of them did not vote for Donald Trump in 2016. Yet they are locked down with a malignant narcissist who, instead of protecting his people from Covid-19, has amplified its lethality. The country Trump promised to make great again has never in its history seemed so pitiful."

O'Toole quoted George Packer's remark in *The Atlantic*: "The United States reacted ... like Pakistan or Belarus — like a country with shoddy infrastructure and a dysfunctional government whose leaders were too corrupt or stupid to head off mass suffering."

Then he stepped back to trace how American ignorance and insularity produced a Donald Trump, who promised to end "American carnage" in his inaugural address yet now revels in all the carnage he has created.

As things get worse, he concluded, "(Trump) will pump more hatred and falsehood, more death-wish defiance of reason and decency, into the groundwater. If a new administration succeeds him...it will have to clean up the toxic dump he leaves behind. If he is re-elected, toxicity will have become the lifeblood of American politics."

It is getting worse fast. As Trump pushes states to reopen so the economy improves before November, his own advisers' confidential studies estimate the level of infection and likely death is three times greater than what the public is told.

"Pity" struck a particular chord with the prideful. But during 53 years as a foreign correspondent, I have never seen so much of that contempt, anger and even loathing among allies who desperately need the values and wherewithal of pre-Trump America.

In the 1920s, a sign above the editor's desk at the *Brooklyn Eagle* read, "A dogfight in Brooklyn is bigger than a revolution in China." America caught onto Hitler and Hirohito far too late.

As the war ended, Americans took the lead to shape a United Nations. They helped rebuild Germany and Japan not as largesse but rather as forward thinking. They kept watch in the 1950s as Stalin's Russia became a fierce foe, and China invaded Korea.

Vietnam was the turning point. After U.S. forces declared victory in 1975 and evacuated in disarray, most Americans tuned out "foreign" news. Reporters provided plenty of it, often at risk, during the '80s and '90s. Only dramatic moments got much attention.

After hate-driven fanatics struck at America's very essence on 9/11, I was sure a critical mass of citizens would start to take notice of dan-gers beyond their line of sight. Instead, most turned farther inward. And now we are paying the price.

With short memories and a need for Republican notables who preach unity, much of non-Trump America has reinvented a kinder, gentler George W. Bush. But I still keep on my desk a plaintive lapel button reading, "Is It 2008 Yet?"

His baseless Iraq invasion and its aftermath killed millions of innocents and squandered trillions of dollars. Torture and heavy-handed tactics by U.S. forces spawned terror groups that have expanded deep in Africa and Asia, with lone-wolf sympathizers who force America and Europe into police-state surveillance.

Bush upset delicate regional balances, which Barack Obama struggled to restore. Bashar al-Assad crushed Syrian rebels as Russians moved in, swelling refugee camps. But diplomacy held Israel in check and brokered a multiparty accord to lower heat in Iran.

Then Trump waded in, biased toward Israel's hard right, ignorant of Iran's complexity and hungry for Saudi wealth. He ignores the world's worst humanitarian calamity, in Yemen. As a result of all this, he risks war with unimaginable consequences.

Trump demanded a Nobel for charming Kim Jong-un into docility. If it weren't for him, he insists, America would be at war with North Korea. In fact, Kim's nuclear threat looms increasingly larger, and he has his fondest wish—to play on the world stage.

Not long ago, economists saw India and Brazil as emerging power-houses along with China and Russia, a bloc known as BRIC, in a prosperous interconnected world. India and Brazil now follow Trump's lead toward autocratic isolationism.

In the end, Trump's signature chunk of raw meat for his masses is what threatens America most, with frightening reverberations across a world that awaits November with trepidation: national borders and immigration policies.

I know the southern border well, having grown up in Tucson just up the road from Nogales. I studied in Guadalajara, worked on a paper in Mexico City and in later years reported on Central American military dictators, guerrillas and drug runners.

No Wall can keep out committed bad asses. Most jobless Mexicans would happily do seasonal work, pay taxes, and return to their families until the next crop. It used to be that way. And why not grant more visas to qualified people who enrich any society?

The problem is universal. Families facing violence, persecution or hunger have no option. Climate chaos, conflict and poverty will swell human tides to overwhelming levels. Sealing borders won't make them vanish. Embittered victims of perceived injustice find ways to get even.

International law requires countries to grant asylum when justified. Sending people home is often a death sentence. Human decency demands giving destitute migrants food and shelter until their situation is clarified. The expense, as national security, is money well spent.

The long-term solution is to help people stay home. Focused foreign aid educates kids, builds infrastructure and fights corruption. Trump's approach is the opposite. He rails against "shitholes" that take our money and give nothing in return.

At one recent "press briefing" rant, he threatened ominously to look into $32 billion in development assistance. That amounts to about 0.1 percent of the GDP, among the stingiest per capita levels of all aid donors. Then he stumbled over the acronym, PEPFAR, clearly clueless about the program he was criticizing.

Bush launched the President's Emergency Plan for AIDS Relief in 2003, $80 billion in public and private funds that saved an estimated 17 million lives by 2018. Trump may not realize it, but it is now coordinated by his good-cop briefer, Deborah Birx.

Covid-19 rages in the Horn of Africa and down into Kenya where unprecedented locust swarms eat up grain that survives drought and heat. Al-Shabab terrorists strike harder as armies are stretched thin. In Zimbabwe, once a rich breadbasket, farmers starve.

For people fixated on problems at home, it is easy to ignore 70 million desperate people on the move somewhere far away. But like the pandemic Trump tried to wish away, the longer we ignore them, the bigger the crisis when they make their presence known.

Depraved-Heart Massacre

APRIL 22, 2020, TUCSON – Donald Trump, shaping fingers into a pistol at a 2016 Iowa rally, exulted: "I could stand in the middle of Fifth Avenue and shoot somebody and wouldn't lose any voters, okay?" Today, it is as if he had blasted away in Manhattan with a machine gun.

For two months, he dismissed the clear and present Covid-19 threat, mocking it to crowds as yet another Democratic hoax. "It's one person from China; we have it totally under control." True believers put their lives at risk—and everyone else's.

Now he rejects any blame in daily delusional ravings—fact-free self-focused hubris—as the virus kills in the tens of thousands. His past actions were perfect. His natural gift for science enabled him to see the pandemic coming before anyone.

"Depraved-heart murder," Wikipedia says, is "a 'depraved indifference' to human life that causes death" whether or not there is explicit intent to kill. It applies if "defendants commit an act even though they know their act runs an unusually high risk of causing death or serious bodily harm to a person."

The case is clear-cut in America. And by scapegoating the World Health Organization, withholding funds it needs to thwart the pandemic and other killer diseases, Trump extends depraved indifference to an entire planet.

He imperiled the nation he swore to protect, ignoring his experts' warnings as he fired up crowded rallies, thumbed inane tweets and golfed. He tried to stop sick U.S. citizens on a ship off California from landing. That, he said, would drive up infection statistics.

After visiting the CDC, Trump told *Fox News* that experts, and also Vice President Mike Pence, wanted to bring the people to shore, but he disagreed. "I like the numbers being where they are," he said. "I don't need to have the numbers double because of one ship that wasn't our fault."

He hurled "fake news" insults at a briefing when asked about *The New York Times'* April 14 investigation by six seasoned reporters with damning details, leaked documents and video. Then he showed a shameless propaganda montage, edited so that Maggie Haberman's words on camera came out as praise for him.

He claims he was the first leader to close borders to Chinese, neglecting to say Americans returning home brought in more virus. That was late January after 38 other countries imposed strict border controls. During February and into March, he continued to mock the threat.

Despite Trump's repeated assertions, just over 1 percent of Americans have been tested, mostly the seriously sick and medical workers. There is almost no contact tracing. As a result, the actual number of cases is far higher than official figures report.

Known cases are fast closing in on one million, one third of the world total. Nearly 50,000 deaths, 17 times the number Osama Bin Laden killed on 9/11, are a fourth of the global toll. This in a country that makes up 4.25 percent of the world's population.

America now tests 150,000 people a day. A study by Harvard specialists says that should be six times higher now and then increase by at least 10 times more during the summer before a likely resurgence in late fall when temperatures drop.

Against all but unanimous scientific advice, Trump is pushing hard to reopen for business. "People want to return to work," he repeats, not adding that his reelection hinges on the economy. He urges his base to "liberate" swing states with Democratic governors.

Depraved-heart murder...is "a 'depraved indifference' to human life that causes death" whether or not there is explicit intent to kill. It applies if "defendants commit an act even though they know their act runs an unusually high risk of causing death or serious bodily harm to a person".

Georgia, which lags far behind safety guidelines, is opening even massage salons, tattoo parlors, bowling alleys and theaters. Governor Brian Kemp, a staunch Republican, forces mayors in Atlanta and Albany to comply despite vehement objections. People from other states can drive in to join crowds at restaurants and beaches.

Even Germany, a model of quick testing, containment and low mortality, is restoring isolation after a cautious reopening. Pathogens are like spermatozoa. It only takes one to slip past protection.

When a novel coronavirus appears, unfazed by antibiotics or vaccines, urgent broad testing is crucial to find infected people so teams can track down their recent contacts. Even if borders are sealed to foreigners, returning citizens bring it home.

But Trump refused German-made tests that WHO provided to Asian and European countries to curb infections and prevent spikes that overwhelm hospitals. Tests also reassure fearful people when results are negative. This is about humans, not statistics.

Bungling and bureaucracy delayed U.S.-made tests for nearly two months. Trump declined to invoke the Defense Production Act, so profiteers sold vital necessities to the highest bidder. States compete with the federal government for overseas supplies.

Meantime, Trump forges ahead on his devastating projects: The Wall, pipelines, plunder of national parks and wilderness. He is reversing limits on air and water pollution that will kill more people in the long run than Covid-19.

He claims absolute power, packing the courts at blinding speed and raising fears that he may attempt to delay November elections. Authoritarians elsewhere use the pandemic to blot out democracy. Terrorists seize the moment to recruit and attack.

After Congress voted to spend $2.2 trillion as emergency relief, Trump fired the inspector general charged with preventing corporate insiders and favored friends from creaming off funds meant for desperate families and struggling small businesses.

A recent exchange at the daily unhinged campaign-rally press briefing defines him.

Yamiche Alcindor of PBS said, "A man's family got sick because they listened to you about the coronavirus," and she asked, "Are you concerned you could have gotten people sick?"

He replied, "And a lot of people love Trump, right? A lot of people love me, right? To the best of my knowledge, I won."

A few days ago, a reporter recalled that Mike Pence promised there would be 4 million new tests by the end of the week, which is more than the total so far. He asked what happened. Trump, oozing condescension, said, "I'll say it for the fifth time. We have tested more than any country."

An NBC poll found only 36 percent of Americans trust Trump to manage Covid-19, just over half of those who trust Anthony Fauci. Clearly miffed at being upstaged, Trump now eclipses him at briefings. He had to disgrace himself by recanting his assessment on CNN: Had the government acted more effectively, lives would have been saved.

Still, the NBC poll showed Trump's approval ratings are unchanged from April 2019: 46 percent for, 51 percent against.

Rejecting bipartisan harmony, Trump heaps scorn on Democrats. He obliges states to beg for federal resources as if they were his own. He claimed absolute power, but then backpedaled. He can take credit for any successes and blame governors for all failures.

Trump pushed hard for hydroxychloroquine, an anti-malarial used for lupus and arthritis. It can't hurt, he said. That spiked the price and limited supply to people who depended on it. Initial studies suggest it is useless against Covid-19 and may increase the risk of death.

After first praising Xi Jinping for transparency, Trump now blames the pandemic on China because it hid the truth. Of course, China is secretive and punishes people for speaking out. It's China. The United States has a higher standard.

He says Barack Obama left no emergency stockpile, a bald lie. Even if that were true, he had three years to restock it. He says he inherited useless tests. As a very stable genius, he might have found a way to foresee a novel coronavirus that surfaced in late 2019.

He calls the outbreak a surprise to everyone. Who knew this might happen? In fact, he was blindsided because he dismantled Obama's extensive global alert network, removed the health expert from the NSC and hobbled U.S. intelligence.

Trump's America-first approach shuns cooperation with well-run allies. *Die Welt am Sonntag* reported that he offered $1 billion for rights to a vaccine being developed if it would be exclusive to the United States.

He also ignores outbreaks in poor countries already facing collapsed food supply. When the Covid-19 pandemic is eventually blunted, it may well live on, endemic in regions from where refugees are forced to flee toward Europe and America.

This horrifies Michel Lavollay, a source I have trusted for 40 years, who knows as much as anyone about pandemics. He was a French volunteer doctor before linking up with Jonathan Mann, an American epidemiologist, to focus on HIV-AIDS.

When AIDS began to run wild in the 1980s, WHO focused on finding a medical magic bullet. But Mann, who did the first AIDS research in the Congo, knew the urgent priority was to stop people from exposure to it.

Lavollay supervised testing when Mann set up the U.N. Global Program on AIDS in 2000. Later, he saw diplomacy from the inside as the French Embassy health attaché in Washington. As a U.N. adviser, he was a confidant of Kofi Annan and Richard Holbrooke. Then he worked with Jonas Salk, who made the polio vaccine available to everyone. As Salk put it, "You don't patent the sun."

This, Lavollay told me, is the first global health threat in two decades not being countered by governments working together with volunteer agencies and private companies coordinated by the U.N. with America playing a lead role.

"No one trusts the United States anymore," Lavollay said. "It's impossible to deal with Trump. Governments and companies fight with each other, driving up costs. Without cooperation, a free-for-all and privatization will take an enormous toll."

After talking with him, I watched Trump head off into an unhinged ramble about how much foreign aid America squanders on Africa. He stumbled over the acronym, PEPFAR, clearly new to him. "You don't know about this," he told reporters. "Nobody does."

In fact, most of them do. George W. Bush launched the President's Emergency Plan for AIDS Relief in 2003, which funneled $80 billion into sub-Saharan Africa. By 2018, it had saved more than 17 million lives and kept countless family units from falling apart.

It was not what Trump calls needless charity to places he terms "shitholes." For all of his faults, Bush knew that unless Africans and other impoverished people were helped to give their kids a shot at survival, "security" anywhere was out of the question.

Today, it is cruel as well as stupid not to cooperate globally against a virulent plague that crosses borders and oceans indiscriminately, exposing unfathomable numbers to lingering, lonely death. That sounds like a definition of depraved-heart murder.

Broken Arrows, Forked Tongues

APRIL 14, 2020, COCHISE STRONGHOLD, ARIZONA – Up here where an Apache chief and an Army general once made peace meant to last, stirring views overlook a diminished America, a money-talks nation in the grip of newcomers who believe it belongs only to them.

Before the road narrows and climbs to forests and rocky peaks, I saw a sign on a shabby ranch house fence: "TRUMP—Keep America First." In today's lingo, that means send intruders back where they came from. Fair enough. Adios, dude.

My t-shirt had a different message. Along with a sepia tone photo of four carbine-wielding warriors in deerskin boots framed by an outline map of Arizona, it read in old-timey letters: "Homeland Security, Fighting Terrorism since 1492."

Apaches and other tribes have been around for nearly a millennium. Spanish missionaries came in the 1500s. This was Mexico until 1853. Arizona has been a state only since 1912. We "white eyes" outsiders are the "aliens."

Today, crisp piney air evokes Cochise's time when cellphones were no-G smoke signals, tweets were for the birds and "fox" referred to a shifty carnivore that eagles ate for lunch. Land deeds were inconceivable. But not only snakes had forked tongues.

That 1871 treaty with the general soon fell apart as people moved West. Ranchers and settlers wanted land. After a renegade band killed a corrupt whiskey seller, the U.S. Cavalry mounted up. Blood spilled again for 15 more years.

I learned the history when I camped here as a kid. Since then, I've watched hubris, greed and stupidity too often misguide American foreign policy. Small incidents trigger big conflicts. At home and abroad, this is far worse than I've ever seen.

Arizona, once blue then red, is as politically purple as its majestic mountains. And it is a crucible of two heated issues as Trump tries to shape America in his own image: Who belongs; and who holds title to natural splendor, scarce water and mineral wealth.

On a break from isolation to avoid the killer virus Donald Trump allowed to run wild, I took a slow ride through Indian country and ranchland I knew in the 1960s.

The old whistlestop town of Willcox was mostly locked down, but at a sparse open-air market I met a crusty coot with a long straggly white beard in a shirt proclaiming him a Vietnam vet. He was still pissed that pacifists stopped America from finishing the job.

"I'm not worried about that virus," he told me, with a dismissive wave, then hacked mightily. I skipped my usual routine—a handshake while asking for a name—and just wrote down Gabby. "I had the flu when I was a kid, and I figure I'm immune."

Gabby echoed what I've heard with resolute intensity since 2016: America needs Trump to make it safe and respected in the world. "He says what he means, no ifs, ands, or buts," Gabby said. "You can oppose him, but you'll find out you're wrong."

Cochise, like Geronimo who fought to the bitter end, was a Chiricahua Apache from sky-island mountains nearby, spectacular rock formations that loom 6,000 feet above high desert, with 375 species of birds. Deer and black bear remain, but jaguars are gone.

Driving up the Chiricahuas, the only Indians I saw were two motorcycles made in Iowa, along with two Harley-Davidsons, all kitted out in Hells'-Angels fashion. Their riders were mild-mannered couples on holiday. We talked pleasantly until I mentioned Trump's inaction on the virus. All four eyed me narrowly and roared away.

At Cochise Stronghold, U.S. Forest Service posters implore visitors not to disturb relics and remains. It is illegal, they say, but also vital so that future generations know what came before them. Yet a forked-tongue president plunders the West outrageously.

To the southwest, bulldozers plow up Tohono O'odham burial grounds and ceremonial sites at Organ Pipe National Monument to build a barrier with no practical purpose beyond firing up Trump's base. It devastates wildlife habitats and fragile desert ecology.

Smugglers tunnel under, climb over or cut through. Most contraband moves through ports of entry in trucks and trains. Drug lords and gang leaders come in the front door with faked documents. Only desperate small bands risk crossing the hostile desert. Yet while a pandemic demands full attention, crews push ahead on the Wall.

New regulators enable miners to gouge out natural beauty on public land. A federal judge has blocked the $1.9 billion Rosemont copper mine on sacred ground near Tucson that would send its profits to Canada. But Trump is rapidly packing appellate courts.

Beyond physical impact, Trump has picked up on the ugliest under-currents in American society. He tells fearful, hateful people what they want to hear. Evidence notwithstanding, they tune out all the rest.

Coronavirus has hit Indian reservations hard, as flu did in 1918. Diabetes, cancer, heart disease and asthma are rife. Health care is limited. "This could be like a wildfire," Kevin Allis of the National Congress of American Indians told the Washington Post. "We could all get wiped out."

As settlers moved into Apache lands in 1861, peace was still possible. But George Bascom, a young lieutenant, falsely accused Cochise of a raiding a ranch and abducting a 12-year-old boy. When Cochise went to meet him with family members in tow, Bascom tied him up in a tent. He escaped alone, seizing hostages after he fled.

Cochise tried to negotiate. Bascom refused. The missing boy reappeared and said his captors were from a different Apache clan. By then, Bascom had hanged Cochise's brother and two nephews. Cochise had killed three hostages. And war raged for a decade.

One trooper's diary summed up the lesson Americans have yet to learn: "Tread on a worm, and it will turn—disturb a hornets nest and they will sting you—So with savage Indians: misuse them and you make them revengeful foes."

Beyond physical impact, Trump has picked up on the ugliest undercurrents in American society. He tells fearful, hateful people what they want to hear. Evidence notwithstanding, they tune out all the rest.

Countless Hollywood westerns portray Apaches as vicious killers, kidnappers and thieves. "Broken Arrow" dug deeper in 1950. It would be skewered today as politically incorrect; Jeff Chandler, smeared in red, plays Cochise. But it shows bitter enemies can find common ground with earned respect and diplomacy.

Tom Jeffords, an Army scout turned government Indian agent, spent months with Cochise, winning his trust. Gen. Oliver Howard rode up to the chief's stronghold and agreed to cede the Dragoon and Chiricahua mountains as protected territory.

But after four quiet years, renegades killed a crooked whiskey seller. Settlers demanded protection from "terrorists." Fort Bowie added reinforcements. When Geronimo finally surrendered in 1886, Chiricahua Apaches were sent to Florida on a trail of tears.

The grim reality of "manifest destiny," as America pushed west against all obstacles, natural or human, helps answer that hoary question about the wider world: why do they hate us?

Cochise and Jeffords often came to mind as I reported on abrupt American policies shifts, broken promises that left allies in the lurch and turned pacified people into adversaries seeking payback. The Kurds, again and again, are blatant examples.

Americans tend to see "primitive" societies as easily manipulated, not realizing that they are committed to codes of honor and blood revenge when wronged. Many are outraged when friends the United States takes for granted refuse to follow it into folly.

No one is "for us or against us" as George W. Bush declared when he widened his response to 9/11 into a diffuse global war on terrorism. That only magnified the threat geometrically and cost well over $6 trillion, money we could use at home about now.

That is ancient history for people who follow their leader in any direction his lies direct them. For them, birthright and tradition count for little. Money and guns prevail. America is first, and nothing else matters.

Land titles, obviously, are now essential. Too many people share limited space, and parents pass on property to their kids. But no one really owns land that has been here for millions of years and will be here when we go.

Cochise took Jeffords and the Army general at their word. Had settlers and soldiers not reneged on their treaty, Apaches might still be up here sharing their land with visitors who respect their ancient spirits.

To Indians, breaking an arrow meant peace. But in a superpower that arms to the teeth and wages needless war, "broken arrow" is now a term for a nuclear weapon gone astray or triggered by accident with devastating result. Something has gone wrong.

A Crime Against Humanity

APRIL 01, 2020, TUCSON – Let's be clear. Deadly plague and deadlier politics put America at more risk than perhaps anything since the Civil War. Only a widespread awakening to reality can prevent COVID-19 from leaving permanent scars in a divided, diminished nation.

Donald Trump's initial mocking of coronavirus—another Democratic hoax after impeachment failed—amounts to wholesale negligent manslaughter. As the toll inexorably climbs, it amounts to a crime against humanity.

As late as February 28, he told a crowded shoulder-to-shoulder rally, "Now the Democrats are politicizing this, and it is their new hoax." Until mid-March, his message to Americans was be calm and buy stocks.

Now he exploits fear and suffering in daily primetime "press briefings," as bald a display of demagogy as I have seen in a half-century of covering despots around the world. Do not be surprised if a Reichstag mysteriously catches fire before November.

If you're new to the Mort Report, this is not what it is meant to be. I'm an up-close reporter who values credibility and objectivity earned over a lifetime. But nothing about today is normal. If seasoned journalists cannot say it straight, we are lost.

I am now back in Tucson where I started out, happy enough in the shadow of dramatic mountains, banging away on a keyboard as chili bubbles on the stove, yet burning to be out there exploring those colors and contours on the big world map by my desk.

Today, a grasping megalomaniac sees that map as a Monopoly board and cons his cultists into believing that he dominates it. Americans who oppose him focus on crisis at home, with scant attention to his global depredations that threaten human survival.

Authoritarians exploit the virus to clamp down. A *Washington Post* headline made the point: "Coronavirus Kills Its First Democracy." Hungarians have fought for freedom since a 1956 uprising. Viktor Orban just dissolved parliament, cowed the courts, cancelled elections and said journalists face jail for what he decides is "fake news."

Before 2017, an American president would have come down like a ton of bricks. Trump is silent. Orban, who slams his doors to refugees despite a long history of other nations protecting Hungarians who were forced to flee, is a man after his own heart.

The threat was clear early in January. South Korea used a German test offered by WHO to screen its population with free drive-through checkpoints. Other countries did the same. With no cure or vaccine for COVID-19, doctors can only isolate and track it.

Today, a grasping megalomaniac sees that map as a Monopoly board and cons his cultists into believing that he dominates it. Americans who oppose him focus on crisis at home, with scant attention to his global depredations that threaten human survival.

Trump said Americans could do better; they couldn't. As the CDC and FDA lost crucial time to bureaucracy, he mocked the "hoax" at rabble-rousing rallies and laughed off "the Chinese virus" on *Fox News*. The virus will magically disappear. He tried to stop Americans on an infected ship off California from returning to their own country. A rising casualty toll would spook the stock market.

When outbreaks across the country forced him to take it seriously, he avoided what people needed most: truth. Anyone who wanted a test could have one. In fact, the few tests available were given to the seriously sick, defeating their purpose.

Trump rewrote history, denying what Americans had seen and heard for themselves, repeated often on newscast and available online. Across the world, people watched in disbelief as he contradicted medical experts, touted bogus cures and boasted that his actions were perfect, better than in any other country.

Americans are inured to this pathological lunacy. We tally up his lies and adjust to a new normal. But this is about the suffering and death of millions, as well as a grim new reality for a planet already facing existential threats.

Real journalists do their job nobly, asking basic questions any real president must answer. One encounter typifies Trump. Peter Alexander of NBC asked, gently, what he would say to Americans who are scared? "I would say you're a terrible reporter," he shot back, with a rant about sensationalist unpatriotic fake media.

Later, real journalists were moved to the back; sometimes their microphones were turned down. Trump called instead on partisan plants, who set him up to complain about how he was so unfairly treated and to explain why he is a very stable genius.

Trump punishes governors who fail to express gratitude for public property he parcels out as if it were his own. He gutted Barack Obama's preparedness measures and global monitoring team yet blames his predecessor for leaving him a "horrible mess."

He spews self-praise and bristles at the mention of countries that acted more efficiently than America, which is most of them.

"I know South Korea better than anyone," he asserted during one performance and said Seoul's population was 38 million. For starters, the 9.8 million people who actually live in Seoul know Korea better than he does.

The United States tested more people in eight days than South Korea did in eight weeks, he said, neglecting to mention that it is five times more populous. And he missed the point. America's increase in testing is far too late.

Even people who oppose Trump tend to take him at his word when he misleads them about other countries. In America, the wider world has long been an afterthought.

Amazon's blurb on William Lederer's *Nation of Sheep*, back in 1961, is still fresh today: "Discusses the effects of the apathy and ignorance of the American people on foreign policy, relations with other nations and use of foreign aid funds."

Back then, the title was apt. Sheep trot behind a shepherd with barely a bleat, but they pause if they sense danger. Trump cultists are closer to Edward Abbey's description of cattle: "shit-smeared, disease-spreading brutes" that stampede blindly when spooked.

Arizona is cattle country. As elsewhere in America, lots of people here have risen to the challenge. The sacrifice of medical and public safety workers is beyond any thanks we can offer. Countless others donate, volunteer time and take risks for strangers.

But gun sales have spiked by a factor of ten. Gov. Doug Ducey includes them as essential to emergency supplies during the pandemic.

The latest outrage is in Trump's fiefdom, Florida, which thrives on the cruise ship industry and tourism. Gov. Ron DeSantis wants to airlift medical help to two ships off the coast. Both, with dead and seriously ill passengers aboard, have been turned away from ports up the Latin-American coast. Out of options, they are desperate.

"We cannot afford to have people who are not even Floridians dumped into South Florida using up those valuable resources," DeSantis told Fox News, after conferring with Trump. The final decision is up to Broward County officials in Fort Lauderdale.

At stake is whether a corner of America under stress will uphold its standard of human decency. History is troubling. In 1939, the Port of Miami turned away the Saint Louis, sending 900 Jewish refugees back to Europe. Hitler exterminated many of them.

Other governors have stepped in, at times pleading for help despite Trump's grudges. Jay Inslee of Washington is "a snake." Gretchen Whitmer is "that woman in Michigan." Andrew Cuomo forced him to delay relaxing social distancing for Easter. Once, miffed at states demanding stockpiled materiel, he replied, "We are not a shipping clerk."

Anthony Fauci says stringent measures could keep the death toll below 240,000 Americans. If nothing had been done, he said, it could surpass 2.2 million. For two months, by pretending there was no threat, Trump did worse than nothing.

The United States of Bubble Wrap

FEBRUARY 27, 2020, CAVE CREEK, ARIZONA · A sign at the outskirts, "Where the Wild West Lives," is hyped up horse flop. Despite old cowboy décor, people in this Disneyesque Frontierland and biker hangout mostly tune out a wider world in their United States of Bubble Wrap.

Like so much of America today, Cave Creek lives in comfortable ersatz reality, isolated from crises and conflict across an increasingly unlivable planet. Apathy condones outrages by elected leaders who in earlier days would have been tarred and feathered.

Cavalry troops wresting land from Apaches built an outpost here in the 1870s. Ranchers and gold miners followed. In 2000, the town, county and state bought the nearby Spur Cross Ranch to protect its 2,154 acres of unique Sonora Desert splendor.

At sunset on Spur Cross, pastels tint the tangled arms of giant saguaro cacti. Trails wind up rocky outcrops sheltering ancient Indian relics. Mule deer lurk in lush sage-scented greenery along the rippling creek. Soon wildflowers will burst into color.

But suburbia encroaches everywhere. Swimming pools evaporate as temperatures soar. Lawns suck up water. Gas-gulping power wagons stand ready to tear up pristine desert not yet bulldozed for new lots. An awful lot of TVs are tuned to Fox News.

In town, the mood is quickly evident. "I don't talk about politics," one young woman told me. Elders tend toward a familiar smirk that delivers a clear message: My brokerage account is doing fine, and I know what I believe. Butt out.

Max Boot captured the national picture in a *Washington Post* op-ed, a twist on the paper's watchword: Democracy Dies in Darkness. "This is how democracies die," he wrote, "not in darkness but in full view of a public that couldn't care less."

Examples are stark in Arizona, a deeply divided state bordering Mexico. Even if a sizable voter turnout in November blends red and blue into purple, natural beauty and priceless cultural heritage have already been irretrievably lost.

Maricopa County, including Cave Creek and nearby Scottsdale, booms as wealthy sun-seeking outsiders move in. Many, in new cowboy hats and boots, regard Mexicans as "aliens" despite Arizona roots that run eight generations deep.

Arizona Republicans love the Wall. They allow miners and developers to destroy wilderness, squander scarce water and obliterate tribal sites held sacred for millennia. They cheer a demagogue president who imperils their children's survival.

Democrats prevail down in Pima County, "Baja Arizona" to old-timers. They see folly in costly barriers that devastate wildlife and Indian graves but fail to stop drugs that go under, over, around, or through them. Still, focused on domestic issues, most pay scant attention to Donald Trump 's global depredations.

When I was a kid in Baja Arizona, most of us reviled Barry Goldwater, a Republican senator who famously declared, "Extremism in defense of liberty is no vice; moderation in pursuit of justice is no virtue."

When people called him crazy, the American Psychiatric Association invoked a "Goldwater rule." Shrinks cannot diagnose someone they haven't examined. Fair enough. Although archconservative, he read the Constitution, respected his oath of office and compromised when necessary. He'd be a flaming "liberal" today.

Trump is different. In Cave Creek, a noted brain researcher passing through summed up what so many psychiatrists see: a bottomless black hole of narcissism that no amount of adulation can satisfy. A man like that is capable of anything.

Reporters don't do clinical diagnosis. But look anywhere around the world for evidence of Trump's impact. Just take countries beginning in "I."

Trump flew to India after Narendra Modi promised him a crowd of 10 million in his home base in Gujarat State. It was about 115,000 in a cricket stadium, and many left during the speeches. He extolled the world's largest democracy where faiths "worship side by side" overlooking Modi's drive to disenfranchise India's 200 million Muslims.

After riots killed 800 Gujarati Muslims in 2002, George W. Bush banned Modi from a Washington visit. As Trump lunched with him in New Delhi, Hindus attacked Muslims elsewhere in the capital. At least 11 people were killed over two days. Muslim victims said police stood by as their shops were set ablaze.

Recently, Modi sent troops to impose strict curfews in Kashmir where India and Pakistan, both with nuclear arsenals, now chest-bump toward conflict. China backs the Pakistanis, who resent Trump's tilt toward India.

In Iran, Trump pushed hardline mullahs to the brink of war because, most likely, the deal to blunt their weapons buildup had Hillary Clinton's fingerprints on it. That reverberated in Iraq, where Shiites moved closer to Iran after Bush's invasion.

The Islamic State no longer has boundaries, but Trump's policies make it more dangerous than ever, with shadowy offshoots in Africa and Asia, along with lone wolves who surface in Europe and America. And then, of course, there is Israel.

Growing anti-Semitism in America is fanned by Hitler-loving louts who chant on occasion, "Jews will not replace us." Elsewhere, it is largely a reaction to Benyamin Netanyahu's one-state plan to colonize Palestine with American support.

In Indonesia, with the largest Islamic population, Chinese largesse blunts objection to brutal repression of a million Muslims Uighurs, a flagrant example of how China expands its disregard for human rights across the world.

The Italian rightwing follows America's example, closing borders to Africans fleeing conflict and crop failure caused by climate change. As Washington slashes aid to countries Trump calls shitholes, desperate human tides swells.

Ireland's border is one of multiple issues in post-Brexit Britain. The United States could help its closest ally, but Trump slammed down the phone on Boris Johnson, who then cancelled a trip to Washington.

Aides said Trump was "apoplectic" because his erstwhile pal allowed Huawei to develop its 5G network in Britain. Johnson, in turn, blames Trump for crippling the world economy with tariffs and trade barriers.

Nothing isolates America from reality. The GOP trump card is a stock market boom doped by tax-cut profits. It took only rogue microbes deep in China to panic Wall Street. The Dow dropped 10 percent in days. We have no idea what awaits as the coronavirus shuts down so much in an interconnected world.

"The West is winning," Mike Pompeo told allies who listened in stony silence at the recent Munich Security Conference in a Germany troubled by disturbing echoes from its Nazi past.

"This is utter hogwash," Simon Tisdall wrote in *The Guardian*, "and almost everyone outside a dishonest, self-deceiving circle of Republican stooges and Trump toadies knows it… In many respects, the US and Europe are further apart than at any time since 1941."

Democratic debates focus on health care, taxes and sniping at one another. Cable channels obsess on small primaries and too-early polls. On *CBS Morning News*, "The World in 90 Seconds," is routinely Trump tweets, minor national stories with dramatic video, sports and late-night comedians.

Young voters want action on climate, but few think through the challenges. Nothing America does alone matters much without a president who can convince China, India and others to put aside national advantage for a common cause.

A smart ex-student of mine synthesized Bernie Sanders' appeal: "We have no functioning government, and everything is on fire, so why not have faith in this man who has always fought for the right things?"

True enough, America badly needs a revolution of the sort Sanders and others envision. Vested interests, sclerotic politics and big money hasten climate collapse and risk unstoppable conflict. A gap widens fast between rich and desperate.

But the Electoral College system is skewed. Hillary Clinton won big in the popular vote, yet she lost. Sanders spooks swing-state conservatives. If he did win, his wish list would consume Congress with little chance of passing.

Like so much of America today, Cave Creek lives in comfortable ersatz reality, isolated from crises and conflict across an increasingly unlivable planet. Apathy condones outrages by elected leaders who in earlier days would have been tarred and feathered.

The question is whether voters look beyond a United States of Bubble Wrap. America needs a president who allies trust and adversaries take seriously, with a firm grasp of global complexities. Prospects are troubling. In Cave Creek, the only mention I noticed of an outside world were Belgian waffles on a breakfast menu.

Joe Biden was sharp, specific and calm in the knives-out CBS South Carolina debate. At 77, a year younger than Sanders and Mike Bloomberg, he is hardly the doddering old fool many call him. Before he was cut off by yet another paid Bloomberg commercial, he outlined smart policy toward China, North Korea and the Middle East.

Biden has made bad calls in the past. As Sanders said when challenged on his own record, all good-serving politicians make decisions they later regret. Good legislators evolve and adapt to a changing world.

Trump's latest lunacies display his despotic intent. He told the Supreme Court, baldly in public, how he wants to be judged. He is suing the *Times* for libel on specious grounds, flouting the First Amendment. Craven Republican senators rubber stamp any excess.

Over the next four years, in my view, America needs to get back on course so fresh new leaders can shape long-term reform. For now, Sanders, Elizabeth Warren, and Amy Klobuchar are already in Congress where laws are made; in November, voters can give them a solid majority, with diverse young newcomers attuned to the times.

Whomever Democrats choose, it is now or never. The abyss between Trumpistan and what America needs to be is as wide as the Grand Canyon up north. Trying to leap across it in a single bound is not an encouraging prospect.

After the "Trial," It Is Now Happening Here

FEBRUARY 11, 2020, TUCSON – After the Senate kangaroo court delivered its verdict, Mike Pence crowed, "It's over." No, it's not. Weapons of mass destruction—Donald Trump's thumbs—have attacked America from within, and they seem to be winning.

Trump, who takes his transparent distortions as divine truth, sees any challenge as lèse-majesté. Americans have less than 10 months to set him straight before another term entrenches monarchal oligarchy— or worse.

Yet Democratic candidates snipe at one another to attract voters guided by emotional impulse as though the most crucial election ever was simply picking a winner on Dancing With the Stars.

The world badly needs the wherewithal and moral compass of an America that works with others to fend off global calamity. But too many voters ignore this big picture to obsess over day-to-day political horseraces and nitpicking sidelights.

Having covered self-obsessed demagogues since the 1960s, I know one when I see one. Some are far less brutal than others, but all have one basis in common: they do whatever they want and take vengeance on dissenters.

Upon acquittal, Trump strutted through the White House behind a military band playing "Hail to the Chief." He heaped praise on his sycophants then spewed vulgar invective and threats at "sick, horrible" Democrats who made his family suffer.

His unhinged hour-long ramble treated assembled Republican legislators like a dog trainer tossing biscuits at his neutered poodles. He lavished encomiums on Mitch McConnell for blocking bills and packing the Supreme Court.

Later, he told reporters that Nancy Pelosi broke the law by tearing up a copy of his lie-laced State of the Union speech, an "official document." It was, he said, "so disrespectful to our country, and actually very illegal."

Payback was immediate. Alexander Vindman, a U.S. Army colonel with a Purple Heart whose family fled the Soviet Union for a country that speaks truth to power, was frog-marched out of the White House under guard. So was his twin brother, an NSC lawyer whose only sin was a family tie.

Last week, I recalled Sinclair Lewis's 1935 novel on how a fascist-minded elected leader in the United States could follow Hitler's path to power: "It Can't Happen Here." Now, William Shirer's *The Rise and Fall of the Third Reich* is more apt.

Shirer quoted an editor in Berlin, close to Hitler, who told him in 1938 that at times the Führer "lost control completely, hurling himself to the floor and chewing the edge of the carpet." Men like that are capable of just about anything.

I mentioned Michael Getler, a wise colleague who two decades ago cautioned me not to underestimate the American people. His correspondent son, Warren, responded to say that his father would have been horrified at today's hypocrisy in Washington.

The world badly needs the wherewithal and moral compass of an America that works with others to fend off global calamity. But too many voters ignore this big picture to obsess over day-to-day political horseraces and nitpicking sidelights.

Warren studied Nazis at Princeton before covering Germany. He remembers journalist Dorothy Thompson who interviewed Hitler and outlined how dictators seize power: fire up less-educated, largely rural workers with xenophobic tropes; scapegoat non-white minorities; discredit the press with big-lie propaganda.

Obviously, situations differ. Hitler exploited fear in a nation crippled by inflation and postwar political turmoil. Trump evokes baseless fears to con workaday cultists as he enriches the ruling class and plunders natural resources.

I first saw despotism at its worst in 1967. Joseph-Desire Mobutu added "Democratic" to Republic of the Congo. Then he Africanized his name, with a ludicrous list of glorifying titles, and ruled by fiat. The thud of rubber stamps drowned out token opposition in his parliament.

My stringer, Baudouin Kayembe, edited a brave weekly that shed light on corruption. He was jailed on trumped up charges and died from what Mobutu called an unfortunate illness. Uncounted millions have been killed in the Congo since then.

Singapore was the other extreme. Lee Kuan Yew, brilliant and ruthless, shaped democracy according to his iron whim. His ruling party groomed future leaders from grade school. Fines discouraged "Western permissiveness." Critics were sued, or worse.

After a leading Chinese-language daily irritated Lee, its publisher got the message and moved to Canada. Singapore today is rich and orderly, a model state for those not troubled by what amounts to a better-packaged North Korea.

Americans once paid more attention to the world. During the Ronald Reagan 1980s, farsighted conservatives began to reshape the society. They started with primary education, as Lee Kuan Yew did, backing curricula that discouraged critical thinking and curiosity about the world.

News was once a one-way feed from reporters who witnessed what they wrote about. Now the internet vastly expands access to information but also gives a false sense of omniscience. People form fixed ideas from whatever sources they choose.

As McKay Coppins reports in *The Atlantic*, Trump's billion-dollar disinformation campaign blurs reality with false stories targeted at specific groups and slimes critical reporters with made-up slurs or damaging details dug up from the distant past.

Overwhelmed by it all, Americans tend to base opinions on impressions of the moment and personal concerns, losing sight of how global currents impact on their lives. Many overlook the complex indirect electoral process that determines who wins.

Logic points to Biden. November will be, as he says, a fight over America's soul. And more, it is about choosing a president who foes take seriously and friends see as a known quantity equipped to thwart an authoritarian trend that Trump encourages.

Germany is troubling again. As Angela Merkel prepares to step aside, the far-right gains strength. Neofascism looms elsewhere in Europe. Iran has been pushed to extremes. Trump's pro-Israel policy inflames the Middle East. Turkey is a wild card on NATO's eastern flank. The list is long, and each case demands proven diplomacy.

But after a clown-car caucus in Iowa, commentators declared that Biden was on the ropes, rejected by voters in one small state. Then a shiny new object from left field and a redoubtable old warrior took commanding leads in the New Hampshire primary.

Age is relative. If some people are past it at 50, others hit hard in their 90s. Bernie Sanders is a year older than Biden, and both are up to the job. But elections hang on a few swing states where wavering Republicans fear the bugaboo word, socialism.

Hillary Clinton has already showed that a woman can win. Amy Klobuchar or Elizabeth Warren would be good vice presidents; both now do vital work in the Senate. A more seasoned Buttigieg can make a strong run in 2024. As for Mike Bloomberg, should billionaires buy elections, skipping the scrutiny of debates and primaries?

Biden shows signs of fraying under the constant eye of crowds and cameras. In New Hampshire, he told a 21-year-old woman who said she'd been to an Iowa caucus, "You're a lying, dog-faced pony soldier." He said later that was a joke, an old John Wayne line.

Video shows everyone laughing that off, and it is hard to know the context. But *Fox News* and late-night comedians made much of it. Like Howard Dean's odd scream of enthusiasm in 2004, it will cost him.

Most young voters, less likely to factor in how the Electoral College works, already dismiss Biden as an uninspiring relic. His TV ads belittling Buttigieg's small-town inexperience and his repeated references to Barack Obama don't help.

At this stage, it's all guesswork—to the Republicans' delight. If Biden is the candidate, the risk echoes 2016. Bernie diehards, Never-Hillary people and apathetic nonvoters put a demagogue in the White House.

Trump, along with his idiot-prince older son and big-money backers, has made his intentions clear. He intends to make America in his own image. For those who oppose him, the lesson is old as Antiquity. If you go after a king, don't miss.

Bloomberg, the dark horse, is coming up fast on a separate track. He is the anti-Trump, an honest billionaire with far better instincts. New

York insiders who knew him as mayor tell me they have doubts. He apologized to those discomfited by his stop-and-frisk policy but not for the principle. He is a money man, focused on results.

Bloomberg's news agency outraged some of its staff by basing editorial judgment on hits and comments rather than editors' judgment of what mattered. One story reporting hard evidence that Iraq had dismantled its banned weapons, the reason for invasion in 2003, stirred little interest. It was not pursued.

It may come down to showdown between two New York rich people with opposing ideas about what is best for America. A benevolent dictator is a much better choice than a malevolent one. But money is not how we should keep score.

Yes, It Can Happen Here

FEBRUARY 05, 2020, SAN FRANCISCO – Michael Getler, perhaps the wisest editor I've ever known, once warned me, "You can go awfully wrong betting against the American people." That rumbling in the background is not the Big One. It's Mike backflipping in his grave.

Even Joseph Stalin feigned more legitimacy than the U.S. Senate's contemptible show trial. The predetermined verdict, with neither witnesses nor documents, gave a mercurial, power-obsessed president free rein to ignore the Constitution.

Donald Trump held up vital aid to an ally at war, seeking dirt on Joe Biden, and then blocked a congressional inquiry. The defense rested on his last call to Kiev: "no quid pro quo." That was after a courageous insider made his extortion public.

John Bolton's leaked manuscript nailed down any niggling doubts. Senator Lamar Alexander of Tennessee called Trump's actions "inappropriate" but not impeachable. Inappropriate is farting in a buffet line. This is more.

Yet much of America shrugged it off, failing to see the incalculable damage done not only to basic values at home but also to a world facing despotic manipulation of "truth," widening conflict and climate chaos that threatens unimaginable consequences.

The Superbowl was great, but we are in trouble when a football game with no real lasting impact draws ten times more television viewers than a sham impeachment.

At the vote to acquit, after Mitch McConnell excoriated Democrats for a baseless partisan pursuit, Mitt Romney alone broke Republican ranks. He said his faith in God would not let him condone "an appalling abuse of public trust."

Getler edited the *International Herald Tribune* long after I left it and then returned to the *Washington Post* as ombudsman. He moved to

NPR in the same role, a wise rabbi-ethicist who understood the fundamental need for a respected, impartial press.

We discussed the draft of my book, *Escaping Plato's Cave*. With his cautions in mind, I worried the subtitle might be alarmist: "How America's Blindness to the Rest of the World Threatens Our Survival." Today, that's an understatement.

Another Trump term would concentrate dictatorial powers in the White House, buttressed by a packed Supreme Court and rubber-stamp legislators. This evokes troubling echoes from the past.

Hitler took power with a hardcore 40 percent minority because the opposition was split. Sinclair Lewis published "It Can't Happen Here" in 1935, and a new edition appeared just this week. An Amazon blurb sums it up neatly:

"A cautionary tale about the fragility of democracy, it is an alarming, eerily timeless look at how fascism could take hold in America. Written during the Great Depression, when the country was largely oblivious to Hitler's aggression, it juxtaposes sharp political satire with the chillingly realistic rise of a president who becomes a dictator to save the nation from welfare cheats, sex, crime, and a liberal press."

If God alone were going to save America, McConnell would have burst into flame when he swore on a Bible to be impartial. Evolution suggests that senators won't grow spines overnight. America's fate hangs on elections in November.

I'm betting with Getler on the American people. But the odds are terrifying. Too many voters rely on emotional impulse, fixating on narrow issues without considering the big picture. Democrats continue to snipe at one another, fortifying Trump's chances.

Beyond reuniting a divided nation, the next president has to convince allies and foes in a world on the boil that America is sane again. This demands skilled labor, with no time to learn on the job.

Borders today are largely only lines on a map. A virus gone wild in an open-air Chinese market creates global alarm within days. Walls don't stop migrants, refugees and terrorists. The world's macroeconomy, like its ecology, transcends all frontiers.

Early in Trump's tenure I argued that impeachment would produce testimony and documents to shed light on his self-serving depredations. I never imagined that craven senators could get away with stonewalling the people they are sworn to serve.

If God alone were going to save America, McConnell would have burst into flame when he swore on a Bible to be impartial. Evolution suggests that senators won't grow spines overnight. America's fate hangs on elections in November.

America First is now closer to America Only, no longer able to lead by example. China ethnically cleanses millions and scorns reporting of that as "fake news." Russia subverts democracies at a quickening pace, sneering at objections from Washington.

In Europe, the United States is more than a laughingstock. Leaders watch in disbelief tinged with contempt as a nation they admired abandons its defense of human rights and freedoms. Elsewhere, Trump's me-first bullying and toadying spark brush fires apt to flame out of control.

For me, the obvious choice is Joe Biden, a respected known quantity across the world. Of course, he is flawed. But he is the anti-Trump: decent, honest and empathetic. And he is most likely to win over wavering Republicans in the crucial swing states.

Bernie Sanders, Elizabeth Warren and Amy Klobuchar are already well-placed in the Senate, where such domestic policies as health care, taxation and gender issues take shape. Others in the race, younger, offer solid promise for the future.

But that's me. There is also that young Iowan who told a reporter: "Biden? Never in a million years." He is 77, and a *New York Times* editorial backing Klobuchar and Warren argued that he was ready for slippers and the back porch.

I just read Marcus Tullius Cicero's essay on whether old men should serve in public office, written 2,100 years ago in Rome. Summed up, its conclusion was: Duh. Why should hard-earned experience and nurtured relationships be needlessly wasted?

At this stage, no one knows what to expect in November. Generalities make for easy but skewed analysis. There is a myriad of Americas, and many of them are isolated in bubble wrap with specific priorities. In most, "foreign policy" ranks low on the list.

One key element of "It Can't Happen Here" was how so few Americans at the time paid attention to the outside world. Today, despite instant access to reliable information from so many sources, that is still true.

Another is that fearful, gullible people are easily swayed by a dema- gogue's simplistic bombast. Big lies, however transparent, become accepted truth if repeated often—and loudly—enough.

Despite impeachment, Gallup says Trump's approval rating has risen to 49 percent. His State of the Union—jingoistic and aimed squarely as his base—drew chants of "four more years." At the outset, he refused to shake Nancy Pelosi's hand. At the end, she tore up her copy of a speech she called "a manifesto of mistruths."

Trump vowed to protect pre-existing conditions in health care; Republicans are in court to do the opposite. He wildly exaggerated progress on the Wall and crime among illegal immigrants. Barack Obama made America the world's leading oil and gas producer. *The Washington Post* counted 31 falsehoods, including the signature claim Trump has repeated 260 times: the economy is the best it has ever been. And so on.

After acquittal the next day, Trump's response was a tweeted meme that suggested he planned to be president forever. Then, mob-style, Don Jr. fingered Romney as a traitor who should be punished.

Iowa gave a foretaste of the obstacles in an election process that borders on lunacy. Five of the Democratic candidates together spent $55 million on advertising and 400 days to secure only six electoral votes of the 270 needed to win the presidency.

On caucus day, people lined up behind the flashiest speaker, sometimes on a last-minute whim. Pete Buttigieg scored twice as high as Biden, and Amy Klobuchar trailed further behind.

News organizations fielded huge teams, squandering budgets that could send correspondents to cover vital world news. An untested mobile app delayed the results. Shit happens. That was enough for Trump to crow about his inept opposition.

We all know the problems. Elections are about money, with an advantage to Republicans who are better at online targeting and working the algorithms. Voter suppression, gerrymandering and the rest play a part.

The only answer is an overwhelming turnout. Opting out with so much at stake amounts to desertion. The key question is who can beat Trump? But another question is no less important: Who can confront global crises most Americans ignore?

It is hard for voters to keep track of all the conflict and calamity that threaten America abroad. But they don't have to. All they need do is put aside narrow interests and rally behind a seasoned candidate who does.

Now or Never: Watching 2020 Insanity from the Seine

JANUARY 08, 2020, PARIS – The Seine, that lovely little river looping through the heart of France, offers an illuminating view on 2020, already playing out as the year that was a defining point on whither humanity. The view is bleak, yet a few French lessons could help tip the balance toward hope.

The French have punched above their weight since obstreperous Gauls confounded Caesar, alternating between imperial glory and ignominious defeat. They've had enough idiot kings. Now a tumultuous, effective democracy can show America what "We, the people" really means.

Entente is easily defined: no good comes from a foreign policy that jabs sharp sticks into hornet nests. France has buried enough millions to know the costs of conflict. Tough commandos fight hard when they must. A nuclear force de frappe delivers a clear message: Don't screw with us.

At home, that holy trinity—liberté, égalité, fraternité—rests on a concept Jean-Jacques Rousseau outlined in 1752: *le contrat sociale*. Money is not how you keep score. Pitched battles today in city streets recall the point of pitchforks at the Bastille: Rich people do not own poor ones.

Down on the Seine, metaphor amounts to fact. If everyone in a sinking boat fails to bail together, they all go down.

World leaders gathered in Paris during 2015 to head off an inexorable slide toward climactic doom. They made solemn promises to take modest first steps and build on those. Despite some progress, an over-all assessment today comes down to the ever-popular expletive: merde.

America has 10 months to jettison a megalomaniac who heats troubled waters to a boil. He spurns human tides fleeing conflict and climate collapse. He upended entente with Iran to spark unwinnable war. He enables China, Russia and others to curb freedoms and cultural diversity.

Christmas was dark this year in the City of Light. Unions paralyzed France in a standoff with Emmanuel Macron over pensions and prices, joined by Gilets jaunes, a diverse movement of pissed-off people in yellow vests. Freelance louts smashed and burned for the hell of it.

Riot cops weighed in with weaponry, abandoning past restraint. A Hong Kong TV crew, inured to mean streets, flew in to cover the story. A police charge put four in the hospital. Trains shut down. Holiday family gatherings, sacred in France, were cancelled. And the strife continues.

One woman, not a protester, was crushed by crowds trying to get home on a rare running metro. "This is total hell, and I hate it," she told a reporter, "but there is no choice. I'm doing this for my kids." Like so many others, she fears Macron and big business will reduce workers to widgets.

The French watch Netflix, and *The Irishman* troubles them. They've had no Jimmy Hoffa, who lived high on union dues and power until he ended up mysteriously vaporized. Labor leaders, bosses and the gov-ernment have always slugged it out toward reasonable compromise.

But 2020 is different. Refugees and migrants strain stressed budgets. Many from the Middle East resist integration, sparking far-right fear and loathing. Radical imams and terrorist recruiters feed on rising tensions. Facebook and the internet harden positions deep into rural France.

Elsewhere in Europe, what Samuel Huntington foresaw as "a clash of civilizations" pushes rightwing leaders to muzzle dissent as they plunder resources. Hungary and Poland, which tore down an Iron Curtain with help from America, have erected stout wire fences with "Keep Out" signs. Italy flirts with a new sort of fascism, with increasing ties to Beijing.

Yet this is still France. Even the rich get basic family allowances so there is no "welfare" stigma, but they pay higher taxes. State universities cost about $185 a year; good health care is mostly free. Courts prosecute former presidents on minor corruption charges. Ninety million visitors come here each year with nothing more untoward than a picked pocket or an iffy oyster.

And yet despite solid firsthand reporting, with news analyses by specialists who understand French complexities, exaggerated headlines and social media echo chambers feed Americans' unfounded fears. Take, for instance, anti-Semitism.

At a recent party in Arizona, a well-heeled matron told me, "I used to love France, but I'm afraid to go now because they hate Jews, and it's so dangerous." I noted that my name was Rosenblum, and I'd reported from there for four decades. With a dismissive wave, she continued on, missing the irony of synagogue massacres and neo-Nazi marches in the United States.

Then I met Hamid, an Afghan toxicologist who sees the world as it is. Anti-Semitism is hardly new in France, but now it is about politics, like Islamophobia. Incidents spiked 74 percent in 2018 over 2017 as Donald Trump encouraged Benyamin Netanyahu's one-state policy. For now, reported verbal and physical abuses number in the hundreds among 550,000 French Jews. If new settlements and repression continue, most likely there will be blood.

Hamid, a neighborhood Mister Rogers, is ready to help anyone with anything except during Friday prayers. His rug-merchant family lived well in Afghanistan's better days. He survived Soviet assaults that destroyed half of ancient Herat in the fertile northwest, then came to America before warlords and post 9/11 conflict did the rest. With his Japanese surgeon wife and a book-loving young daughter, he blends well into the American melting pot.

"Islam is not a violent religion," he said. "The *Quran* teaches kindness to strangers and respect for a world created by God. I have a word for what people preach when they deviate from this with their personal interpretation: Hislam." Their fanaticism, he said, provokes hatred for a religion with well over a billion peaceable followers.

That struck a loud chord. Bigots draw few distinctions. Jews are Jews, even those who believe that Israel's future depends on sharing land according to negotiated accords with equal rights for all. Ignorant xenophobia breeds fast. "What's next?" Hamid asked. "The Chinese?"

I've reported in nearly every part of the Muslim world. I ran the AP bureau in Indonesia, by far the largest Islamic country, along with Malaysia. I roamed other non-Arab Muslim states in Africa and ranged widely in the Middle East.

Muslims, Christians and Jews were People of the Book. Even when war clouds gathered over Israel, I frequented mosques and visited homes on holy days across the Islamic world. Apart from run-ins with secular authorities, I was welcomed as a stranger at the door.

In France, I hung out in tough exurbs where Muslims from ex-colonies lived on the edge. Once, I joined a group slaughtering lamb on Eid al-Adha, which honors Ibrahim (Abraham), who was ready to sacrifice his son at God's command. A few guys began to hassle me until they picked up my accent. "You American?" one asked. "You should have said so. We love Americans."

That changed fast after George W. Bush invaded. Now, under Trump, I watch my back, not only in Muslim countries but also in those tough French neighborhoods. For hothead Hislamists, a Jew is a Jew, just as so many Americans make no distinction among Muslims.

For those who believe in signs from on high, flames rising above Notre Dame Cathedral on the Seine were as clear as Moses's burning bush. The Almighty is not pleased. For others, simple reflection is enough. History, if ignored, does worse than simply repeating itself.

The last war Americans had to fight for their freedom started in 1939 when Hitler invaded Poland. Unchallenged by Washington, his tanks overran an unprepared France. The United States responded only after Japan left it no choice, late in 1941.

A wiser America helped Europe emerge from the remains. NATO and the United Nations held the line against a Soviet threat until, in the 1990s, the world had a shot at working together to find lasting peace and prosperity.

Back then, power was about nukes and naval fleets. Today, that is illusory. Afghans and Iraqis beat America to a standstill with home-made explosives and guerrilla tactics. Nuclear wars leave no winners. Peace demands skilled diplomacy led by seasoned heads of state who keep their word. Young voters need to understand that experience and earned respect matter.

In today's diverse world, no one gets to say who is right or wrong. Societies do what they do. Empty threats and missile-rattling only worsen crises until they are unsolvable. Foreign aid, hardly largesse, is essential to security and cheap at the cost. Most people on the move would rather stay home in cultures they know with friends and families. If they can't, they won't.

People with the right to choose their own leaders can no longer take that for granted. Nothing today is more important than real news from reliable sources that allows citizens to make smart choices.

From the Seine, I watch deputies head to the National Assembly with furrowed brows. No Mitch McConnell stymies democracy, flaunting bias before evidence is heard. Coalitions form and shift. Voters hold toes to the fire. When outraged, they swarm the streets and hurl paving stones.

Presidential campaigns are short and cheap; no one can buy the office. Candidates get equal TV time, one after the other, drawing lots to determine the order. In a first round, people vote their consciences. Two weeks later, after the top two sandblast each other in face-to-face debates, a winner emerges with a clear idea of the national mood.

French-style democracy is hardly perfect, but it is worth a close look. At the very least, Americans might note the first words of La Marseillaise: "Citizens, On Your Feet!"

III. DOWN THE RABBIT HOLE

Down to Bedrock

JANUARY 29, 2017, TUCSON - This one is personal. No thunderbolts from the mount by an old-croc correspondent. I'm just trying to fathom how a petulant spoiled 5-year-old grabbed the helm of a noble ship of state and immediately steered it onto the rocks.

Forget economics and politics; the issue is our humanity. Long ago, some bureaucrat chose to label non-Americans as "aliens." And now, in a matter of days, we have alienated most of the 7 billion people who share our imperiled planet.

The irony is bitter. Peter Turnley circulated a haunting photo of our Statue of Liberty. He and I watched Romanians face gunfire to topple a tyrant. We've covered heartless despots from Bosnia to Somalia. Now the brutality is here at home.

An admiring France gave us that statue. With a theatrical pen stroke, Donald Trump smashed it to rubble, slamming our doors in collective punishment of innocent victims whose lives we've shattered and others defined only by their nationality.

Trump condones torture. Never mind that it doesn't work. It is monstrous. Elected representatives shrug it all off, busy with plans to make the rich richer, to destroy natural heritage, to impose authoritarian control over the bodies of constituents they're sworn to protect. Others with integrity have to stand up.

This is still America. The ACLU rallied a judge to spare those few with visas from being sent home. But who knows what they and so many others, now face from a vindictive chief executive who detests being thwarted.

Many Americans proclaim that Trump is not their president. But he is.

Like it or not, we are now defined by the fearful, hate-filled, self-focused or simply gullible who showed up to vote while so many others had something better to do.

Half of Trump voters, an *Economist/YouGov* poll says, believe Barack Obama was born in Kenya, likely a Muslim, and Hillary Clinton ran sex slaves out of that Washington pizzeria.

The worst among them pledge allegiance to Hitler.

I understand the greed. We've seen people shove their way to a buffet table, grab the last shrimp, and smirk at those who, with more civility, waited in line. Losers. We've read *Lord of the Flies.*

Some people with more money than they could spend in 1,000 years see wealth as only a way to keep score. Like those pigs in *Animal Farm* that believe some species are more equal than others, they plunder a planet at risk of climatic collapse.

But how can a deluded fringe believe we are somehow safer by telling 7 billion "aliens" we are better than they are and raining hellfire not only on actual enemies but also innocents trapped among them? That is exactly what feeds terrorism.

Forget economics and politics; the issue is our humanity. Long ago, some bureaucrat chose to label non-Americans as 'aliens.' And now, in a matter of days, we have alienated most of the 7 billion people who share our imperiled planet.

Our U.N. ambassador, fresh from the confines of South Carolina, tells 192 nations we are taking names if they don't "watch our back." What naivety and arrogance. The United Nations is a forum for friends and foes to find common ground.

Grand geopolitics are not complex when you see them as simple human interaction writ large. If you ran China or Russia, and a hothead American president with a nuclear arsenal peppered you with mixed messages, what would you do?

As we saw with Saddam Hussein and Muammar Qaddafi, tin-pot tyrants who call our bluff are forced to hold out to a dramatic end. What happens if one of them, in Pyongyang, say, has a nuclear missile that can reach California?

Israel is key. It has a right to exist and is vital to keep the unholy land stable. Yet if we support hard-right zealots who colonize land legally attributed to others, and we condone massive military overreach, the eventual result is too horrific to imagine.

I write these reflections 60 miles from a border I've known well since I was a kid. Trump wants to spend what can't be less than $45 billion to wall us off from rich cultures our country has lived with in symbiosis for centuries.

The Wall is insane. As a top ex-DEA chief notes, smugglers amortize a million-dollar tunnel with a single drug run. They use ultralight aircraft and catapults. Migrants with a will always find a way. In fact, more Mexicans now head south than north. Central Americans seek asylum, not clandestine passage.

Still in its talking stage, the wall is already impacting U.S. businesses as Mexicans boycott them in protest.

And so on. There is much more to say.

Those millions who poured into the streets last week are a promising start. People who seldom thought about the democratic process are mobilizing, meeting, and flooding their senators and congressmen with demands for accountability.

By now, every citizen who cares knows what to do. Congress is crucial but so are state legislatures and local authorities at every level. We need to defend honest news organizations and box in police who exceed their authority.

At the heart of it all is a simple question: Who are we?

My own conclusion is that if enough of us demonstrate basic humanity and common sense, if we do what is essential to protect generations to follow, the America we know is safe. If not, we are fucked, and so is the world beyond.

Trump, Months on the Job, is Already at War – With America

JUNE 6, 2017, PARIS - The risk was high that Donald Trump would provoke a war somewhere, but who imagined it would be against the United States? And if more of us Americans cannot overcome stupidity, cupidity or simple apathy, he could win.

For a year now, I've put a lifetime of reportorial objectivity on the line to write what seem like increasingly shrill jeremiads about this man who knows no shame or restraint, with no loyalties or higher purpose than feeding his insatiable id.

This is real. I have not mistakenly dropped trompettes de la mort mushrooms into my morning omelet. But if I sound like Chicken Little with hair on fire, tune me out. Verify facts in their actual global setting, and draw your own conclusions.

Trump's aides evoke Godfather mafiosi—"going to the mattresses," as some of them put it—as they impede scrutiny of blatantly improper ties to Russia and outrageous conflicts of interest. His earlier attempts to silence James Comey defied belief.

Jeff Sessions, a mean-spirited little bigot with extremist views, disregards his own recusal. A legal fig leaf might protect him from perjury charges, but he is Attorney General. Perception matters in a society based on public trust.

Mitch McConnell, a mean-spirited slightly larger bigot with extremist views, enabled Republicans to pack the Supreme Court. Congress is hardly likely to impeach Trump. New laws threaten prison terms for constitutionally guaranteed dissent.

The administration's Robbing Hood approach to taxes—take from the poor and keep it—widens beyond future redress an abyss between the rich and the desperate. It also frees up yet more money to further unbalance a corrupt electoral system.

In ignorance or by willful intent, Trump distorts a non-binding consensus by every nation but Syria (and Nicaragua, which wants tougher measures) to confront climactic change that is making Earth uninhabitable. His bombast increases the terrorist threat by geometric proportions.

He says the world will laugh at us if we don't get tough. The world stopped laughing months ago. Our friends now despair and seek alliances elsewhere. Our foes hate us with growing intensity.

Imagine how we look to Britons, our closest allies who followed us into the Iraq war, which spawned the terrorism that just hit them hard. Trump directed a cheap-shot tweet at London's respected Muslim mayor as he struggled to restore calm.

Yes, many small investors are racking up profits because irrational exuberance is back in the stock market. But few of those promised jobs are materializing. Smart money managers expect Wile E. Coyote to look down soon and plummet earthward.

This all could go either way. News organizations detail every outrage. Responsible legislators raise hell. Lots of worried citizens protest.

But unless a critical mass at local and national levels leads to landslides in 2018 elections, we're toast.

Starting now, we need to stand up and holler. Elected and hired civil servants—in particular, the president—have to understand their job descriptions, the source of their salaries, and the consequences of abusing authority.

We cannot blame "the media" or "politicians" or other indefinable collectivities if we've lost touch with reality. Just as reporters do, citizens have to seek solid sources, test them against hard data, and believe only their own eyes and ears.

Slow-moving coups follow a classic pattern…They start with fearful people who believe preposterous exaggerations about outsiders in their midst and bogus bogeymen who would do them harm.

While we focus on the daily circus, a fox-in-the-henhouse cabinet quietly allows oilmen and miners to destroy wilderness, pollute waterways, provoke earthquakes, and blast away at those purple mountain majesties.

Beyond a human toll, the Islamic State commits crimes against humanity by plundering ancient sites held sacred by local civilizations. We are doing the same thing to Native American land in the Dakotas, at Bears Ears, and elsewhere.

Consider that human toll. Proposed healthcare "reforms" will kill far more Americans than terrorists can. The Congressional Budget Office details how badly the poor and elderly would suffer, financially as well as physically.

People outside the United States constantly ask me why so many Americans fight so hard to deprive their countrymen of medical care, a fundamental right everywhere else. Is the answer really blind greed and callous disregard for the plight of others?

Domestic politics are not my forte, but I've have spent half a century abroad watching democracies vanish, sometimes overnight. Most often, citizens resist, and many end up dead in the streets. Rarely do people simply let it happen.

Slow-moving coups follow a classic pattern, and we are halfway down that road. They start with fearful people who believe preposterous exaggerations about outsiders in their midst and bogus bogeymen who would do them harm.

Legislators back despots-in-waiting for their own purposes, ignoring their oaths of office. They pass laws - or condone executive decrees - that allow draconian control over citizens. They assume, correctly, that few people notice until it's too late.

After Trump's inauguration, Washington police swept up hundreds of protesters, along with journalists and bystanders. Some were charged with felony rioting, faced with long prison terms and $25,000 fines. This blipped briefly on the radar then faded away.

With charges added later, defendants could be liable to prison terms of 80 years. However prosecutions play out, the upshot is ominous. It is hard to keep tabs on authority. Demagogies take police at their word and skip individual due process.

In the end, it comes down to simple integrity, and our president has next to none. Look at this from any angle you choose. For me, with roots in Arizona, the defining symbol is that insane Wall.

Sean Spicer recently showed reporters pictures of a silly little structure he claimed was the border barrier near a town southeast of Tucson he mispronounced as Nayco. In fact, a high dissuasive fence runs past Naco and along most of the frontier.

Half of smuggled contraband comes through ports of entry in trucks or trains. People on foot who manage to sneak in carry little in backpacks across hot, dry desert. The net flow of Mexicans now heads south, not north.

Trump's pharaonic erection would give tens of billions to contractors, including his business buddies. It would dislocate families and impact wildlife. But it would bedazzle the hardcore that keeps on buying his bullshit, no matter what.

That is his gamble. He can count on his committed, even if it is a minority, because the rest of us are too disheartened or disorganized to stop him.

After the London Borough Market attack, Trump stripped away niceties with an in-your-face tweet from the mattresses in his war room: "People, the lawyers and the courts can call it whatever they want. But I am calling it what we need and what it is, a TRAVEL BAN!"

Surprise; he lied. What his lawyers claimed was merely non-specific extreme vetting of travelers from a half dozen Muslim countries was a blanket rejection of people who can help us overcome alienation among a faith shared by 1.8 billion people.

This is the Trump who boasted he could shoot someone on Fifth Avenue and not lose his zealots' support. It is the man who insulted Angela Merkel but heaps praise on a Turkish tyrant and a Philippine mass murderer who sneered at an invitation to our White House.

Now, at war with values that are basic to America, he flouts his insatiable id and dares us to do something about it. In fact, we can do plenty.

Trump's grand plans are stalled among partisan politicians who know what happens when an aroused rabble bangs on Bastille doors. We need to bang louder, daily, as if our democracy depended on it. Those elections next year may be our last chance.

Sinking Into Trumpistan

NOVEMBER 28, 2017, PARIS - I am just back from two polar opposite nations. One, a model democracy, is rich in resource and spirit; the other, benighted and self-obsessed, is an oligarchic quasi police state. Both share a misnomer: United States of America.

Disunited, the world's lone superpower risks rendering Earth uninhabitable, sparking uncontained war, and ceding global leadership to authoritarian China. At least a third of Americans seem neither to know nor to care.

The president's jihad on news coverage allows government and business to plunder in plain sight. "Tax reform" is Robin Hood in reverse, stealing from the poor to give yet more to the rich. Dumbed down public schools entrench complacence.

A handsome woman named Eva, whose neatly applied eyeliner does not mask signs of a hard life, put this in focus near Columbus Circle in New York, where a brooding high-rise is labeled in letters no one can miss: Trump International Hotel and Tower.

"Don't talk to me about Donald Trump," she said, in a brand-name haberdashery on Broadway. "He didn't elect himself. Now you have to live with that." Then she stopped herself and went back to ringing up my new shirt.

Eva did not ask me to omit her last name, but foreign correspondents soon learn when it is necessary to protect people who speak frankly. In the new America, this is too often the case.

She escaped Albania in the last days of Enver Hoxha, whose paranoiac tyranny left him with only China for an ally. In New York, she taught herself English, raised her kids, and spoke her mind without a thought to consequences.

Today, recalling the bad old days she fled, she is cautious with strangers. But when I asked about familiar people and places I had encountered while covering post-Hoxha Albania for *Associated Press*, her eyes moistened and she opened up.

Although she despises Trump, Eva notes that the world has lots of sociopaths with an unquenchable thirst for adulation. For her, the calamity is that after a year of lies and destructive policies, his hard-core remains, and resistance cannot coalesce.

She fears that apathy, ignorance and selfishness are pushing a noble nation backward toward the truth-twisting despotism that people elsewhere suffer and die to overturn.

I looked hard for a view that speaks for the other America. In a complex country of 320 million people, a reporter can only listen to multiple voices in different places and then zero in on those that reflect the essence.

In the end, I settled on a married couple, well-educated filmmakers who worked in the Reagan White House and now live in the wilds of Virginia. Trump is not perfect, both acknowledged, but they say he is making America great again.

Asked how, the husband replied, "He cleaned up Obama's mess." In a year, he said, Trump has spurred a flagging economy and boosted employment. His wife nodded, but both declined to discuss actual statistics. They agreed on a label for Hillary Clinton: crook.

The conclusion seems clear. Those who inform themselves by have-it-your-way "news" are deaf to reason. Unless a critical mass of others who separate prejudice from reality outvotes them, the damage could well be permanent.

Few Americans, I found, see how closely all societies are linked in the wider world. Trump's America First campaign has pushed other countries toward new trading patterns. Politically, they shift their alliances and allegiances. Overall, the impact is incalculable.

Take energy independence, an Obama policy that Trump now pursues with a vengeance. Whatever its short-run economic benefits, it is not only devastating to the environment at home, but also destabilizing much of the world.

Ecological damage was already severe when new "regulators" scrapped the few safeguards Obama left in place. They targeted wilderness areas, Indian sacred sites, and fragile ecosystems. Aquifers and waterways lost vital protection.

Now lower fuel prices mean Americans burn more gas in bigger cars, pumping yet more carbon dioxide into the air. Only the United States spurns the Paris accords. At climate talks in Bonn, its tone-deaf envoy was booed for pushing "clean" coal.

Collapsed prices have crippled Venezuela and inflamed terrorism in Nigeria. Russia, hit hard, had amped up intrigues in Europe. And now, as Saudi Arabia repositions itself to diversify from oil, U.S. foreign policy abets its depredations across the Middle East.

U.S. airpower helps Saudis pound neighboring Yemen back to the Stone Age. U.N. officials say 11 million children face acute risk, starved by a month-long blockade as they face the world's worst cholera epidemic. The civilian death toll climbs above 8,000.

A single ship was allowed to dock late in November with a month's food for two million people, relief agencies said, but 18 million face dire need in a mountainous country more than twice the size of Wyoming.

Beyond Yemen, scores of desperate millions seek refuge from war and climate chaos, for which America shares substantial blame. U.S. policy accepts only token thousands, after severe vetting. John Kelly, ex-general and designated adult in the White House, wants none at all.

Trump's pro-Saudi stance is uniting Iran's moderate factions with hard-liners. He repudiates a hard-won accord with Western powers, China and Russia to limit Iran's nuclear capacity. The billion-dollar U.S. air-base in Qatar is crucial to operations across the Mideast and South Asia, but the emirate is now struggling, isolated by its Gulf neighbors.

As these and other intertwined global crises worsen, amateur ideologues hamstring a State Department gutted of seasoned diplomats. My own longtime contacts are all but unanimously livid. Some quit and publish stinging comment.

As Washington turns inward, Chancellor Angela Merkel keeps a firm hand on the Atlantic Alliance and keeps Vladimir Putin at bay. Germany opposed the Iraq War that left so many homeless, yet she took in a million refugees. Now her job is in play as an extreme Germany-First faction amasses power. Without her, we are deep trouble.

In the Far East, Trump pursues his playground shoving match with another mercurial narcissist who is perfecting a nuclear warhead that threatens California. And he is still trying to wall off Mexico, ending a centuries-old symbiosis.

America's non-stop TV news channels make scant mention of the world beyond the oceans that isolate it or growing authoritarianism at home. Instead, they focus on Trump's distractions, braggadocio and serial insults.

The president's jihad on news coverage allows government and business to plunder in plain sight. 'Tax reform' is Robin Hood in reverse, stealing from the poor to give yet more to the rich. Dumbed down public schools entrench complacence.

Clearly, these are more than random brain farts. Trump is a gifted con man. While he captures people's attention with outrageous sideshows, his minions pick their pockets. He is changing national policy on everything from net neutrality to plundering the oceans.

Beyond America, this sparks reaction ranging from consternation to contempt, along with laughter at what America has become. France Inter, a countrywide radio network, offers a new comedy feature: Trump's most ridiculous tweets.

That storm over LiAngelo Ball's shoplifting arrest in China sounded like an Andy Borowitz spoof. Trump claimed he saved the UCLA basketball player from a decade in jail; he was furious when Ball's father did not thank him.

"It wasn't the White House, it wasn't the State Department... IT WAS ME," Trump tweeted. He called Ball "an ungrateful fool" and, with racist overtones, "just a poor man's version of Don King, but without the hair."

In fact, China was unlikely to have jailed LiAngelo at all, legal experts say. In such cases, foreigners are routinely sent home to avoid a diplomatic morass. American justice today can be far harsher, and the world notices.

The British daily, *Independent*, featured a long piece in November on how Washington police swept up nearly 200 protesters at Trump's inauguration and charged many of them with felonies that could mean 60 years in prison. Most were eventually set free, but a freelance photojournalist is now on trial.

The broader backdrop is harrowing. Americans are now often presumed guilty, and justice is no longer blind.

Linda Greenhouse, the redoubtable courts expert at the *New York Times*, now a visiting scholar at Yale, wrote an opinion piece headlined, "A Conservative Plan to Weaponize the Federal Courts," She exposed a Republican proposal to double or triple the number of judges in the federal Courts of Appeals, thus packing them solid.

"In my reporting days, I tried periodically to get my colleagues to break the journalistic habit of identifying federal judges by the president who appointed them," she wrote. "It was just wrong to imply... that judges who were simply doing their job as they thought best were carrying water for their political sponsors, I would argue. I never made much headway. I'm not sure I would make the same effort today. A weaponized judiciary poses real dangers to the legitimacy of the federal courts, and there's no point in pretending otherwise."

Before leaving America, I joined a panel at Yale on where the assault on truth is taking us. Jason Stanley, a philosophy professor who just published *How Propaganda Works*, gave a hair-raising analysis of how big lies and twisted truth can easily undermine democracy.

Jeff Ballou, *Al Jazeera* bureau chief in Washington and retiring president of the National Press Club, outlined how governments across the world use Trump's fake-news onslaught to muzzle not only their local press but also foreign correspondents.

A chilling overview came from Timothy Snyder, whose slim book, *On Tyranny*, lists 20 increasingly familiar aspects of a despotic state. A democracy, he said, falls from within. If it is weak, hostile powers can help it over the edge with a small push.

So here's a fun fact: Snyder noted that Russia spent less to meddle in U.S. elections than the cost of a single tire on a U.S. F-35 stealth fighter —somewhere in the low thousands. It helped to have a candidate who was eager for the assistance.

Reasoned analysis suggests that Trump, if not impeached or compelled to resign, will be humiliated in 2020. But that is in one America. In the other, big-lie propaganda and apathy among eligible voters could give us a different America: Trumpistan.

EXTRA! French Poodle Bites Puffed-Up Yank in the Ass

APRIL 27, 2018, WILD OLIVES, FRANCE - Just back from America, I lit up the TV to hear a presidential president, in complete English sentences free of personal pronouns, tell Congress how the United States was destroying a world that badly needs its leadership.

Emmanuel Macron hit all the right notes, hammering away at every tenet of Donald Trump's twisted us-first jingoism. He played French poodle for two days, lavishing faux-adulation and kissing cheeks. Then, when it mattered, he bit his host in the ass.

A tweet from Madelaine Albright caught the irony: "It has been too long since a President delivered a speech in Washington about the need to defend democracy and support international cooperation."

Macron banged away at his central theme, linking the Iran deal, Syria, trade, desperate people on the move, and all the rest.

"Isolationism, withdrawal and nationalism" prevent common answers to global threats, he said. Without updated alliances the vital institutions America built—the U.N. and NATO—could collapse. Authoritarians would quickly fill the vacuum.

"Your role was decisive in creating and safeguarding the free world," he added, "The United States…invented this multilateralism. You are the one who has to help to preserve and reinvent it."

Macron's zinger—"There is no Planet B"—brought all but partisan diehards to their feet:

"Some people think that securing current industries and their jobs is more urgent than transforming our economies to meet the challenge of global change. But we must find a transition to a low-carbon economy. What is the meaning of our life, really, if we work and live destroying the planet, while sacrificing the future of our children?"

If Americans were not too caught up in their own theater of the absurd to take in Macron's message, and if the French weren't so tied up in knots of their own making, I'd have uncorked a bottle of Côte Rôtie and gone to bed happy.

Instead, I communed with my best non-breaking news source, Emiliano the aged olive tree, who is struggling to recover from the weirdest winter in memory: biblical rains and a hard freeze after prolonged deadly drought.

Up in Paris, a houseboat just hit something sharp on the Seine's bottom. The river is suddenly disastrously low, after months of freak flooding that peaked at 12 feet above normal. Any farmer knows the gravity of such unpredictable extremes.

But Trump is immovable. He excluded Democrats from Macron's White House visit. At a press scrum he called on a *Fox News* stooge to pitch a puffball so he could yell at congressmen who dared to question his dubious top-level staff appointments.

Nonstop cable babble, meantime, focused on which particular women Trump had boinked, overlooking the fact that he is screwing an entire planet. Climate and food security are only part of it. Look, for instance, at Macron's home ground.

I flew back early, just missing yet another strike that has already cost Air France nearly $500 million. Then I drove down; featherbedded train crews are snarling traffic at least until June, throwing the economy—and daily life—into a spin.

Macron, a 40-year-old financial rock star who rode in on a landslide last May, dropped to Trump popularity levels in the fall, and is now just under 50 percent. Detractors say that, like Trump, he wants to curb workers' rights to reward the rich.

This matters to us all. France is among the last brand-name nations that temper their capitalism with "social contracts." Employees expect to be regarded as more than widgets and raw material on companies' books.

Nicolas Sarkozy led France to the right, but voters dumped him as too high-handed and not presidential. He now faces trial for corruption and influence peddling linked to his campaign. Francois Hollande tried to soak the poor but then reversed himself.

The balance is precarious. France is indulgent with crippling strikes, but patience is growing thin. Students are protesting education reform, with stricter entry exams, and leftist leaders threaten a reprise of those 1968 battles in Paris streets.

And this comes back to America. French universities are free, and so is health care. The socialist gulag Republicans sneer at could be a model state if extremes on both sides found common ground. But a transatlantic tug to the right inflames the left.

Macron went to Washington on behalf of the European Union. Trump snubs Angela Merkel, weakened at home because she took in so many of the refugees that America uprooted yet refuses asylum. Fascists in the EU want a Fortress Europe.

Macron's zinger: '...we must find a transition to a low-carbon economy. What is the meaning of our life, really, if we work and live destroying the planet, while sacrificing the future of our children?'

This is far bigger than personalities and individual states. Macron is right: Despots seize on every opening to reshape the world into something ugly and dangerous, with a muzzled press, cowed populations and plunder of global resources.

And yet too many Americans miss the point. Even the *New York Times* mostly blew off the Macron visit, playing it at the bottom of the front page, or inside, with a focus on Melania, pomp, and dandruff.

In France, dailies were also low-key, partly because the French expect so little of Trump. Some dwelt on restored grandeur after the George W. Bush era, when Bart Simpson laughed them off as "cheese-eating surrender monkeys."

Le Monde's lead story revealed how the Islamic State burrowed into Syria and Iraq to exact taxes and infiltrate businesses. By one estimate, it has 15 years of cash reserves. *Le Figaro* and *Liberation* detailed how Trump policy fuels anti-Semitism.

Back in America, too many people ferociously defend worldviews based on fragments of information from dubious sources that confirm personal bias. Even solid news organizations can only sample events and trends that imperil us.

We need to step back to assess what is at risk—and why. This takes time and commitment. But how else do we choose leaders who understand the real world and then hold them to their promises? In sum, we need to grasp context and history.

Start with an immensely readable pair of books by Yuval Noah Hariri, an Israeli who gets it. The first outlines how we evolved from slime. The second outlines how we might avoid reversing the process: *Homo Deus: A Brief History of Tomorrow.*

Terrorists, Hariri writes, are like flies seeking to destroy a china shop. They can't. But if they enrage a bull, it does the job for them. In 2010, terrorists killed 7,697 people, few of them in rich countries. Obesity and related illness killed three million. Coca-Cola is far more dangerous than Al Qaeda.

ISIS was spawned by U.S. torture during the Iraq War, and it spread in the chaos that followed. Local forces, with U.S. and allied support, took back its territory. Now it is a swarm of flies that depends on that bull. You see where I'm going here.

Trump, if ignorant, is hardly stupid. "Terrorism," a perfect bogey, enables him to undo democratic guarantees and freedoms that go back two centuries. He only needs his deplorable base and apathetic non-voters in crucial states to be reelected.

Hariri's thesis applies to all that matters, from income inequality to nuclear threat to climate chaos. The more we allow Trumpian lies, misconceptions and flip-flops from past positions to stand, the more his fake narrative hardens into ineluctable reality.

On Friday, Trump arose early and picked up his dumb phone. He ignored huge news from Korea to tweet yet again about James Comey, who did more than anyone to get him elected. Then he congratulated himself for doing what South Korea and China did to find accord with Kim Jong-un. Mainly, they deflected Trump's shoving match.

What happens next involves intricate diplomacy taking in not only the Korean Peninsula but also the South China Sea and Asia beyond. Think about U.S. policy shaped by John Bolton, Mike Pompeo and clueless warmongers in Congress.

If I've worn out that Edmund Burke quote—"Evil triumphs when good men do nothing"—consider Albert Einstein: "The world will not be destroyed by those who do evil, but by those who watch them without doing anything."

That was Macron's message in Washington. As some fear in France, he may suffer from Napoleon envy, and he likes being in the saddle. But, neither a fool nor an egomaniac, he knows the difference between a horse's ass and a horse.

Mort Report Extra: The Ghost of Common Sense

OCTOBER 08, 2018 - *"Common sense will tell us, that the power which hath endeavoured to subdue us, is of all others, the most improper to defend us."* – Thomas Paine

This is an urgent plea to everyone I can reach. Please pass it on to every American you know before November. Non-voters make up our largest bloc. Others are undecided, and sentient Republicans are wavering. No election in history, anywhere, has been more crucial.

We saw last week how deeply hypocrisy and prostitution now permeate our government. Smart young people offer promise, but if we do not vote now, it will be too late for them. An apathetic, ill-informed electorate will have squandered democracy by default.

If the Mort Report is new to you, I'm a correspondent who has covered world news for 50 years on seven continents for editors who demand strict objectivity. Like all real reporters, I am obsessed with getting facts straight and basing analyses on observation, not opinion.

Until 2016, I'd have cut off a left toe before presuming to tell people how to vote. But I've watched Donald Trump for decades, and I know a heartless would-be despot when I see one. During his campaign, it was clear he would attempt a coup d'etat. With a corrupted Republican Party and enough blind cultist followers to sway an election, he threatens not only our democracy but also the survival of our planet. Please keep reading; this is not hyperbole.

Climatic chaos is real, already affecting food supply. The Intergovernmental Panel on Climate Change just reported temperature rise could reach the 1.5-degree Celsius tipping point within 12 years. To keep our planet habitable, carbon emissions must be cut by 100 percent before 2050. Trump denies it all, pushing coal and fossil fuels as if there were no tomorrow.

Erratic foreign policy risks global conflict and unstoppable cyber-invasion. We can't win a war of attrition with China. We are abandoning our historic defense of human rights and the free exchange of truthful information. We are silent when governments murder journalists.

A calculated spike in prosperity achieved under the Obama administration misleads too many. As Tom Friedman put it, if you burn your furniture to stay warm in winter, you have nowhere to sit in spring. Wile E. Coyote may have already looked down; Nasdaq plummeted on Thursday and Friday. In any case, wealth doesn't matter on an unlivable planet.

The Kavanaugh process shed blinding light on a perverted America. Trump called Christine Blasey Ford "a very credible witness." Later, he mocked her cruelly to delighted laughter from his cult. He is like those black balls with a window on top that deliver a different message every time they're turned over. Far from stupidity, this is cunning calculation.

Trump lied in saying an IRS audit prevented him from revealing tax returns. Then he stonewalled. A New York Times investigation now tells us why. He began with a half-billion dollars of his father's evaded taxes. He cheated, used mob tactics, borrowed from Russians who continue to influence him. When his "very stable genius" failed him, and his father did not bail him out, he declared serial bankruptcies at others' expense.

We've had incompetent presidents before but never one so self-serving and palpably unfit. *The Washington Post* tallies an average of eight lies or inaccuracies a day since he took office. The 25th Amendment or impeachment require a Congress that puts the people's interest above its own. Either would elevate a religious fundamentalist committed to rich donors.

For Republicans, Trump is manna from heaven, a snake-oil salesman who cons the masses. They have systematically crippled the IRS to help themselves and the tax cheats who fund them. Dodged taxes amount to what we spend on helping the poor.

Democrats are disorganized, with leaders who waffle. But at this turn in our history, this is not about parties. Only a crushing, humiliating landslide by one can force change in the other.

Paul Krugman, a Nobel laureate in economics who warned about Trump from the start, interpreted the *Times'* findings with spine-chilling clarity: "Our trend toward oligarchy—rule by the few—is also looking more and more like kakistocracy—rule by the worst, or at least the most unscrupulous. Corruption isn't subtle; on the contrary, it's cruder than almost anyone imagined. It also runs deep, and it has infected our politics, quite literally up to its highest levels."

While we were transfixed by the Kavanaugh saga, Paul Ryan led a House vote to make tax cuts permanent, which would add $3.2 trillion to the deficit over a decade. It may fail in the Senate, but it is a clear sign to rich donors. The fix is in.

Republicans need a Supreme Court majority to protect the Citizens United decision, an Orwellian-named license for big money to subvert democracy. Trump needs Kavanaugh's expansive view of presidential powers. The court can now overturn the dual-sovereignty doctrine that allows states to prosecute cases even after a federal pardon. As Robert Mueller probes deeper into Trump's ties to Russia, that could be crucial.

As it turned out, Dr. Blasey Ford's courageous testimony made the debate about her. Republicans said a good man was convicted without proof. Trump gave the FBI only enough leeway to give the appearance of investigation. Agents did not talk to three of Kavanaugh's Yale buddies who in a *Washington Post* op-ed said he lied about drinking to oblivion. They skipped interviews with the accused and the accuser. And this was not a trial.

An appeal from 2,400 professors at nearly every law school in America had nothing to do with sex or beer. Nor did a condemnation by retired justice John Paul Stevens, a Republican who had backed Kavanaugh. It was about what we all saw for ourselves: a partisan, intemperate man, unable to control his emotions, who blatantly threatened political payback.

Roger Post, former Yale Law School dean, said Kavanaugh would step down if he cared about the Court's integrity and independence. "Judicial temperament is not like a mask that can be taken off at will," he wrote in an essay. "It is in the DNA as is well illustrated by Merrick Garland, who never once descended to partisan rancor despite the Senate's refusal even to dignify his nomination with a hearing." Kavanaugh's "savage and bitter" screed, he concluded, incredibly marks the public mind and undermines America's commitment to rule of law.

Senator Susan Collins of Maine defended her support by shifting blame and ignoring the central issue: "(The) process that has become so dysfunctional, it looks more like a caricature of a gutter-level politi- cal campaign than a solemn occasion." A man is innocent until proven guilty, she insisted. Her stand was different on Al Franken, who she helped drive out of the Senate without an investigation.

Joe Manchin, the only Democrat to vote yes, told reporters he believed there was an assault, but nothing proved it was by Kavanaugh. He avoided the key issues of temperament and partiality. With only a narrow edge in West Virginia, he opted for staying in the Senate.

Trump's priorities at home shame us. Hundreds of millions are being diverted from cancer research to fund private lockups for thousands of children taken from their parents at our borders. There is so much else. But I worry more about his impact abroad, largely unnoticed as American television focuses on his daily antics at home.

His agenda makes some sense on the surface. We should control bor- ders. China has been gaming us for years. North Korea is a potential threat. Trade accords like NAFTA have problems to work out. But his courses of action almost invariably provoke worse blowback.

Russia matches our nuclear capability, but Putin is not after global murder-suicide. He undermines democracy in America and Europe with cyber-attacks and—here the term is apt—fake news. With Putin's mysterious hold over Trump, we do little to stop him. We badly need NATO for strategic planning and intelligence, yet Trump treats partners like deadbeat vassals.

The Chinese, as everyone but Trump knows, don't like losing face. Bridling at his threats, China has gone from an economic rival to military adversary ready for a High-Noon showdown. Trump calls developing nations shitholes and limits aid to the few states that back his policies. That allows China to recolonize Africa, securing raw materials, minerals, oil and U.N. votes with no regard for human rights or official plunder. It is building bases and deploying warships to mark new territory across the globe.

We are already fighting for access to the vital South China Sea, now dotted with Beijing's flags on manmade islands. American bluster makes little impact when U.S. warships collide into one another, killing their own crewmen. The other day, U.S. and Chinese destroyers nearly collided. When tensions run high, accidents or miscalculations can be calamitous.

The Chinese, as everyone but Trump knows, don't like losing face. Bridling at his threats, China has gone from an economic rival to military adversary ready for a High-Noon showdown.

In the Middle East, Trump plays checkers on a backgammon board. His policy on Israel imperils its future as sympathies for Palestinians grow. He gives Saudi Arabia and the Emirates free rein against an infuriated Iran that pre-Trump diplomacy nearly brought out of its shell. Few Americans know the suffering we condone in Yemen, but our allies and enemies do.

Europe had united with open borders and common policies. Now it is dangerously destabilized, with Russia breathing hard from the east. Diehard Fascists in Germany, Italy, Hungary and beyond love Trump's brand of faux-populism. They reject refugee tides from Africa and the Middle East, against whom America slams its doors. Imagine the potential outcomes if we continue to ignore the reasons why so many are forced to leave their homes.

Trump-think is based on a selective view of human beings. Non-Americans (aliens) are lumped in catchall categories rather than as individuals in diverse collectives. This makes us our own worst enemy. "Muslims" aren't terrorists. They're a largely peaceable collective of 1.8 billion people. When zealots among them preach terror, we react indiscriminately. Innocent deaths create new terrorists in geometric proportions.

Announcing his candidacy, Trump singled out Mexicans: "They're bringing drugs. They're bringing crime. They're rapists and some, I assume, are good people." That still defines his border policy.

This mindset disgusts friends and emboldens foes. When a U.S. president tells sovereign states that it is his way or else, most prefer the or else. If strong-armed, as Canada was, they wait for payback. A nuclear-tipped superpower needs a leader who understands world realities. Celebrity status—whether it's a Donald Trump or an Oprah Winfrey—is not enough. This is serious business.

In the end, the fault lies with Congress, which enables and abets Trump's depredations. In the Kavanaugh vote, only Lisa Murkowski of Alaska put principle ahead of her place at the trough to defy Mitch McConnell, who ramrodded confirmation after blocking Obama's compromise nominee for a year.

I first noticed McConnell in the 1980s when Ronald Reagan supported rightwing death squads in Central America as "freedom-fighters" against communism. CIA agents helped them smuggle drugs to Florida. John Kerry, then heading the Senate Foreign Relations Committee, tried to stop organized murder of students, clerics and others suspected of leftist sympathies. McConnell thwarted congressional action. Since then, I've kept watch on him.

When McConnell was a kid, polio threatened to cripple him for life. His parents found public largesse to cure him. Now he moves heaven and earth to torpedo the Affordable Care Act. He vowed to make Obama a one-term president. Failing at that, he opposed Obama at every turn, whatever the cost to America.

In a Madame Secretary episode, the Tea Leoni character sought congressional approval to waive stringent rules to rush food to 250,000 starving Somalis. She spoke to a senator who so resembled McConnell that he could have worn a nametag. Well, he drawled, Congress has to protect farmers. (Rules say food aid must come from American stockpiles, shipped from a domestic port under a U.S. flag.) Then he offered an exception if his Senate pals could use a Pentagon plane for an inspection tour abroad—to Cabo San Lucas where they had to examine an eroding coastline near a golf course.

If even TV writers show us blatant reality that reporters and news analysts detail every day, America ought to notice.

This self-serving bias explains Kavanaugh. When women confronted McConnell as he got off a plane, he stared straight ahead and marched on. "We will not be intimidated by these people," he said later, "There is no chance in the world that they're going to scare us out of doing our duty." They? That's us. McConnell declared his prejudice before witness testimony. With blinders imposed by the White House, the FBI did not corroborate ancient history only a victim would recall.

McConnell's Senate speech dwelt on how a Democratic plot wrecked a noble man's life. He skipped the nominee's disqualifying partiality, which united America's legal profession in opposition. It was a stunning performance, complete with outrage at those importuning women. How dare American citizens tell their elected representative what they think?

And yet people like McConnell are returned, term after term, because not enough voters take the trouble to use Trump's signature words: You're fired.

This administration grotesquely undercuts everything we are supposed to be, from Stephen Miller, the weird 33-year-old automaton who imposes inhuman suffering at our borders to cabinet secretaries who destroy parks, wilderness and natural resources—and so much else.

There is no accountability. Trump is a civil servant on a short-term contract. He owes us daily accounts of what he does in our name, particularly when he vacillates constantly and thumbs policy decrees in cryptic terms via mobile phone in the early dawn. Sarah Sanders went three weeks in September without a briefing. Trump had become more accessible to reporters, she said; she wasn't needed. There was truth to that. Her gross distortions shed little light. We depend on anonymous leaks, suspect at best, and accept that as a new normal. It's not.

Danger looms of a convention to redraft the Constitution. Only 34 states are needed to call one; 28 are now committed. Kakistocracy could take over, with neither checks nor balances. This is no skirmish, as Charles Blow wrote in the *Times*. It is war.

Expect anything, even what would have seemed like paranoia two years ago. A "Presidential alert" recently lit up cellphones across America, a test of a national system for the White House to warn Americans of a sudden emergency. Like a terror alert in November?

The Reichstag is burning. If we do not start dousing the flames in November, we can only blame ourselves for the smoldering ruins.

Here are links to the *Times'* investigation, the *Post's* fact checks and the IPCC update:

https://nyti.ms/3gr6Zgv

https://subscribe.washingtonpost.com/newsletters/#/bundle/factchecker?method=SURL&location=ART

https://on.natgeo.com/2FYaz5q

The Mort Report is a voluntary endeavor by a lifelong correspondent and friends to help connect the dots in an imperiled world. Neither a blog nor advocacy, it is firsthand reportage and fact-based analysis. Share, if you wish. If you'd like to subscribe or contribute to help with reporting and production expenses (thank you), please email mort.rosenblum@gmail.com. More at www.mortrosenblum.net

By Now, Climate Denial Amounts to Mass Murder

DECEMBER 05, 2018, PARIS - Sometimes it seems as if I've banged out a trillion words over the last half-century in news dispatches, books and assorted screeds. None, I believe, are more important than these.

Let's be clear before it is too late. Any government leader or corporate executive who flouts irrefutable evidence of climatic shifts is complicit in murdering the human race.

Nobel laureate Paul Krugman called willful denial of climate change "depravity" in a *New York Times* essay on heedless greed and hubris. That's not the half of it.

Bill McKibben, in *The New Yorker,* outlined in devastating detail what he has watched closely since sounding the alarm 30 years ago. Yet as fire, flood and famine steadily worsen toward Endgame, the world dithers.

"It's now reasonable to ask," he wrote, "whether the human game has begun to falter—perhaps even to play itself out."

As people obsessed on a flash of street mayhem in Paris, few noticed wise old David Attenborough speak gravely in Poland: "If we don't take action, the collapse of our civilizations and the extinction of much of the natural world is on the horizon."

Crocodiles and cockroaches will survive as temperatures rise, but humans will be among the first to go. When? Does it matter?

In the worst case, babies born today may need Dune suits to distill their sweat for a drink of water. Millions already besiege northern borders as crops fail and fishing nets come up empty. The poorest will go first, but the rich will follow.

Back in 1981, the Associated Press gave me a sizeable budget and free rein to prowl the planet in search of underreported crises that matter.

I wrote story after story about climate. Most papers routinely spiked them.

I asked Ben Bradlee at the *Washington Post* for advice on how to interest editors. "I'll put environmental stories on the front page when water is up to my ankles in the newsroom," he replied, only half joking. That was, if I remember correctly, on the third floor.

In 2013, I talked about my book, *Escaping Plato's Cave*, to students at Georgetown University, describing what I'd seen from a hilltop in Tobago: Mud from Venezuela's Orinoco River turned the blue Caribbean brown, and blowing African dust tinged the once-clear air beige.

Some smug kid raised his hand. "I don't think so," he said, presaging an era of alternate facts. Ten minutes online provides anyone validation to form an opinion on anything, regardless of observable reality.

Then in 2015, I covered that crucial Paris meeting. Delegates lauded non-binding accords that fell far short of what was needed. The U.N. "Convention of the Parties" is known as COP. But COP-out is closer to it.

Another COP, number 24, is now meeting with scant news coverage in Katowice, a polluted city in a country that burns carbon for 80 percent of its energy. In a grotesque sideshow, the United States is promoting "clean coal," an unproven, hugely expensive process to capture emissions.

China, now the worst carbon polluter, limits damage at home by fouling environments elsewhere. It exports coal power plants to poor countries, strip-mines, clear-cuts forests and loots endangered global fisheries.

But principal blame falls on Americans, who allow an amoral, immoral president, supported by corrupt congressmen, to ignore what is happening before our own eyes and plunder as if there were no tomorrow.

A fresh report from 13 U.S. federal agencies foretells calamity. Donald Trump tried to bury it over the Thanksgiving break. Then he offered his view: "I don't believe it." He is, he said, too intelligent to accept findings based on four years of analyzing hard science.

In American fashion, the report emphasized the dollar costs of delay. These, of course, are incalculable. McKibben cites a 2017 report by 90 scientists: Arctic warming could mean $90 trillion in economic losses within this century.

Those climate stories we once ignored are now so ubiquitous that most of us simply tune them out. Like taking too small a dose of antibiotics for too long, we're immune. But what we don't know is killing us.

In the end, money counts for nothing when oceans flood coastal cities and islands while unsupportable heat kills off us homo sapiens.

We know how we got here. ExxonMobil and its predecessors hid its own findings since 1977 that fossil fuels were poisoning the planet. Since then, Big Oil has spent hugely to con the public and buy legislators. Now we know better, yet sales of monster trucks and Chevy Subdivisions (a Dave Barry coinage) spike whenever gas prices dip.

Alternative energy is already much cheaper than burning carbon, even without factoring in the trillions that fire and flood will inevitably cost. But effective action must be long-term. Elected leaders, needing votes and campaign funds, seldom think beyond two, four, or six years.

As Trump the con artist knows, people resist sacrifice in the short run for future gain. Yet without firm concerted action that transcends all borders, we are cooked. Humanity is rushing headlong toward extinction.

Trump is a godsend to plunderers like Brazil's Jair Bolsonaro, who calls climate change a Marxist plot and is itching to send bulldozers into the Amazon rainforest. Big and small nations alike are fast reneging on their Paris commitments.

As McKibben wrote in that *New Yorker* piece, which should be required reading before anyone is allowed near a voting both, world leaders in Paris drew a line in the sand, then watched a rising tide erase it.

Here's a thought: If that 2015 U.N. conference didn't provide an answer, consider Paris today. A quarter-million Frenchmen put on yellow vests and showed Emmanuel Macron the limits of presidential power.

It comes down to this. At the rate we are going, we are stealing our children's world. No leader, elected or otherwise, has a right to poison their air, burn their forests or destroy their croplands, much less plunder the world's common ocean.

Those climate stories we once ignored are now so ubiquitous that most of us simply tune them out. Like taking too small a dose of antibiotics for too long, we're immune. But what we don't know is killing us.

A Coup Attempt, Plain and Simple; It Could Succeed

FEBRUARY 19, 2019, TUCSON, ARIZONA - Donald Trump's Wall is illusory, but the writing on it seems clear enough. He is plotting a coup d'etat, gambling that divided Democrats, media sycophants, big money and people who don't vote will enable his cult to make him a modern-day Mussolini.

Trump might watch next year's elections play out as a disgraced has-been on the sidelines, perhaps behind bars, as Elizabeth Warren predicts. But that is a wishful long shot. If he is re-elected, America will find itself tested to a degree that is hard to imagine.

I've covered countless putsches since the 1960s. Military takeovers are swift, often bloody. Subverting democracy takes a lot longer. Either way, they require three essentials: fear of external threat; a rewarded ruling class that undercuts institutions; bullshit that buries truth.

Trump himself sketched out his scenario in singsong mockery when he elbowed aside Congress to confront his bogus border emergency. Legal challenges will work their way up past uncompromised judges to a Supreme Court that Mitch McConnell has allowed him to pack.

Robert Mueller has already nailed six Americans close to Trump, along with 26 Russians. Andrew McCabe says Rod Rosenstein worried enough that the president might be Vladimir Putin's stooge to suggest on two occasions that he wear a wire into the Oval Office.

That alone would oblige a real president to clear himself of suspicion and determine whether America's fiercest foe was perverting its elections. Trump condemns "a ridiculous partisan investigation" and repeatedly tweets "NO COLLUSION!" as if it were only about him.

The irony is breathtaking. A president who spouts a dozen untruths a day dismissed what he called Democrats' falsehoods-in fact, official reports from U.S. agencies—that most drugs are smuggled through ports of entry. "It's wrong," he said. "It's just a lie. It's all a lie."

Despite overwhelming evidence from veteran enforcement authorities, environmental scientists and historical experience dating back to ancient China, he declared: "Walls work 100 percent."

Quality newspapers beaver away, reporting hard facts to the fraction of Americans who read them. Most people, instead, exchange dubiously sourced "news" on their phones when not obsessing on sports, celebrity follies and freak weather they don't link to climate chaos.

On network television, profit supersedes public service. Ratings rule. CBS, which once gave us Murrow and Cronkite, featured McCabe on *60 Minutes*. Yet *CBS Morning News* undercut McCabe's 21 years of established credibility with Sarah Sanders' distorted slurs.

Military takeovers are swift, often bloody. Subverting democracy takes a lot longer. Either way, they require three essentials: fear of external threat; a rewarded ruling class that undercuts institutions; bullshit that buries truth.

One recent morning, CBS ignored crucial news to dwell on a week-old story about a guy who fended off a mountain lion. Next up for citizens starting their day in an imperiled republic was "The Doctors." The host's opening line: "Do you get an erection when you poop?"

Which brings us back to Trump. He toadies up to dictators he admires. Rather than call out Xi Jinping on human rights, he lauds his solution to drug dealers: executions. And to distract from trouble at home, he beats on war drums with dire threats, risking global conflict.

Chest-bumping with North Korea, then Iran, falls somewhere between stupid and insane. Yet old GOP foes join in for their own political survival. Marco Rubio ("Little Marco," who called Trump a con artist) now takes it upon himself to threaten an invasion of Venezuela.

Watch this space for analyses of how U.S. foreign non-policy strengthens China and Russia, while fortifying hard-right parties across

Europe. India, the world's largest democracy, is sinking fast into authoritarianism. For now, America's existential crisis is at home.

Reporters are manhandled not only by goons at Trump rallies but also by police at the Capitol when they seek comment from legislators who represent that increasingly forgotten cohort at the heart of it all: we, the people.

Overweening authority combined with so many people who make snap judgments without weighing details create a polarized society in which extremists thrive.

A Slate dispatch just went viral under the headline: "11-Year-Old Arrested After Refusing to Stand for Pledge of Allegiance." That was in Lakeland, Florida, a year after a school massacre fired up national outrage over America's new directions.

In fact, police said the boy was arrested because he was "disruptive" and "made threats" while being sent to the principal. School authorities faulted a substitute teacher who didn't know that pupils are not obliged to stand for the pledge. They said police, not the school, decided on an arrest.

According to Slate, the substitute teacher asked the kid, "Why, if it was so bad here, he did not go to another place to live?" The answer is easy enough. Zealots don't get to redefine America according to their own biases.

A Supreme Court justice wrote in 1943: "If there is any fixed star in our constitutional constellation, it is that no official, high or petty, can prescribe what shall be orthodox in politics, nationalism, religion, or other matters of opinion, or force citizens to confess by word or act their faith therein." There are, he added, no exceptions.

That was when America was fighting its last unavoidable war. When it ended, wise U.S. presidents repaired a broken world. They helped rebuild Germany and Japan into democracies that now do much to protect an imperiled globe from Trump's repeated abuses.

Here is more of that breathtaking irony. Trump-think flouts America's wealth and military clout with patriotic fervor as if those aspects were what mattered. That is fast destroying what actually makes America great: a history of defending human values.

With luck, I've got it all wrong. Much of America still works as it should, and smart young people are trying to fix insoluble problems bequeathed by us elders. But ask any teacher who stays in an under-paid, underappreciated profession about the bulk of today's students.

Like the economic successes for which he takes credit, Trump in-herited conditions that make America vulnerable. Since the 1980s, wealthy oligarchs have gutted public education to widen the gulf between a privileged few and the workaday majority.

It is hard to blame kids for wanting stuff flaunted everywhere in a society so focused on itself. A hedge fund tycoon just paid $250 mil-lion for a Manhattan apartment, a year's salary for 5,000 teachers who might inspire critical thinking about America and the world beyond.

And yet Trump brought cheers of "U.S.A.!" in his State of the Union speech with an audible-to-all dog whistle: "Tonight, we renew our resolve that America will never be a socialist country!"

What is it about that word? We live on social media. Rich matrons are socialites. Even during McCarthyism, neighbors gathered for pie socials. But add the suffix "ism" or "ist" and even America's 99 percent freaks out.

Socialism is a wild-card word. France under Francois Hollande was hardly a communist gulag. Soviet socialism defined a capitalist system that George Orwell parodied in *Animal Farm*. Pigs ruled, walking on two legs. Some animals were more equal than others.

In essence, it simply means a system in which the rich allow the poor to have enough so they can live decently without having to take what they need by force.

Fascism, as Webster defines it, is more precise: "A political philosophy, movement, or regime that exalts nation and often race above the individuals and that stands for a centralized autocratic government headed by a dictatorial leader, severe economic and social regimentation and forcible suppression of opposition."

Last year someone on Facebook paired pictures of Trump and Mussolini, almost mirror images of men with jutting set jaws, and I-own-the-world gazes. I laughed at the captions: Il Duce and Ill Douche. Today, that is a lot less funny.

The I's Have It – And We All Pay the Price

JUNE 10, 2019, NAPLES, ITALY - You can still get to Sesame Street from here and just about everywhere else in spite of Donald Trump's attempt to wall it off. So as Big Bird might have it, this dispatch about countless global crises is brought to you by the letter "I."

Put aside 25 other letters in the alphabet and consider only what is happening behind that single capitalized vowel.

Iran, Iraq and Israel are at risk of accidental Armageddon. India's demagogic Hindu nationalist leader plays chicken with Pakistan. Indonesia faces climate calamities and Islamist zealotry. Iceland, warming fast, may soon be Rockland. Ireland now has a border to protect.

And here in the heart of an Atlantic Alliance that just commemorated victory over Nazis and Fascists 75 years ago, easy-going Italy is making a sharp right turn. Matteo Salvini, vice premier, is gaining popularity fast by blaming Italian woes on migrants and liberals.

This is no time for America to obsess about itself. Yet the pronoun, "I," and its inseparable partner, "me," define thinking today in the White House, the Senate and among much of an apathetic electorate. A cohesive worldview has sunk into whatever.

I often liken Trump to Mussolini, but even many Italians who fear a return to fascism say that is unfair to Il Duce. He was no fool, they argue. When he put Italy first it was more than an excuse to bilk the poor and fatten up the rich. Nonetheless, he ended up hanged by his heels.

Viewed from Europe, Trump seems more like a Charlie Chaplin caricature of Hitler, a puffed-up martinet enraptured with himself. But unlike Hollywood's Little Dictator, Trump has the means to trigger unstoppable conflicts and thwart global efforts to keep Earth habitable.

It is too early to worry much about Italy, with its entrenched family values and uncanny ability to get through just about anything as long as the coffee and grappa hold out. Those I-states in the Middle East are the real threat.

Before Trump rattles any more missiles, he needs a ten-minute briefing on what happened the last time someone invaded Iran—and on how Iran's 27-century-deep Persian roots underlie a sophisticated society that belies stereotypes about extremist ayatollahs.

Trump Mideast Diplomacy

Even if John Bolton's usual chest-bumping doesn't ignite war, it solidifies hardline leaders. Crippling sanctions on a complex nation of 81 million only embitter moderate and Western-oriented Iranians eager to reconnect with the wider world.

Sanctions mean Iran has fewer funds to underwrite proxy guerrilla armies, but deepening hatreds increase their fervor. Low-cost weaponry and simple terror devices can take a heavy toll.

The "horrible Iran deal" that Trump excoriates was hard-won progress, linking the United States, Western Europe, Russian and China in joint diplomacy to pull Iran back from a headlong rush toward a nuclear arsenal.

Trump's reaction is likely because Hillary Clinton was instrumental in negotiating the deal. It allows for de-escalation without unenforceable ultimatums. Sending troops that could spark hostilities is among the dumbest moves of an administration that excels at dumb moves.

In 1979, Ayatollah Khomeini routed the Shah, who took power in 1953 after American and British agents engineered a coup against a popular prime minister who nationalized Iran's oil. Saddam Hussein seized on the revolutionary upheaval to storm across the border.

For eight years, despite increasing American, Soviet and French military aid to Saddam, Iran fought Iraq to a standstill. Human waves of Koran-clutching volunteers faced air assaults and heavy artillery. The death toll among combatants and civilians soared above a half million.

The war cost Iraq $687 billion. Iran's naval blockade, missile attacks and air strikes all but paralyzed shipping in the region. More than 500 commercial ships suffered damage. When it ended, Iran spent billions arming for any subsequent future threat.

And now Trump, clueless, tweets: "If Iran wants a fight, it's the official end of Iran." As with North Korea, his unhinged non-policy of alternating sticks with carrots has turned slow, steady diplomacy into a high-stakes game of liars' poker.

The world is moving on. While Trump invented cheering crowds in a Britain that largely reviles him, then avoided the gaze of Normandy war heroes, Vladimir Putin embraced Xi Jinping in Beijing. After wary coexistence, they are bosom buddies with a common nemesis.

In Italy, as elsewhere, people ask how Trump gets away with what Robert Mueller made blindingly clear. How can he obstruct justice, condone Russian meddling, overstep authority, weasel out of taxes and promote personal interests? The answer is easy: no one stops him.

And that takes us back to *Sesame Street.* It's not about money. The cost to taxpayers is chump change for a president who has squandered $106 million on golf holidays. He knows that the writers make young people think, and Big Bird is onto him.

In the 1980s, the show savaged Ronald Grump, who bulldozed a neighborhood to build a Grump Tower and yelled at evicted residents who protested. In 2005, Oscar the Grouch, who lives in a garbage can, lauded Donald Grump for having the most trash in the world.

When Trump targeted *Sesame Street* in 2017, Jimmy Kimmel responded in a monologue: "That show teaches so many things he needs to know: which thing is bigger than the other, how to spell, the importance of telling the truth and sharing, listening to others. Maybe throw in some 'Schoolhouse Rock!' He could find out how government works."

Plenty of i-words apply to America's man who would be king, including apt if uncharitable adjectives that start with "ig" or "im." One reflects a distressing reality: incumbent. But there is also that keyword, which looms larger by the day: impeach.

If Democracy is a Spectator Sport, the Good Guys Lose

JULY 12, 2019, PARIS - I've struggled not to say this, even to myself, but Democrats stand a growing chance of condemning the world to Donald Trump's impossible dream: a greed-based oligarchy in America with authoritarian rule bent on stamping out truth.

Too many Americans see democracy as a spectator sport, and they obsess on inside baseball—domestic issues—rather than real-world crises. If candidates continue to snipe over details, the worst president ever could win by default.

In Hong Kong, two million people just jammed the streets, some facing 10 years in prison for storming government headquarters, to force concessions from China. That is as if 90 million people marched on Congress and the White House.

In the United States, half of eligible voters don't even bother to cast ballots. Among those who do, Republicans rally behind the party choice, no matter who it is. They share ideology. Democrats are prone to stay home if not inspired by a candidate.

A society that cannot trust its lawmen and detention officers is sick to its core. That old question recurs: Why do 'they' hate us?

"If this doesn't change, it doesn't matter who the candidate is," author Max Brooks observed recently on Bill Maher's *Real Time*. "If we don't come together now, we're dead."

America is now beyond politics. An unhinged megalomaniac thwarts a global effort to keep Earth habitable, and he fans conflict that could trigger unstoppable war. At his elbow, John Bolton outdoes Peter Sellers as Doctor Strangelove. Yet the last Democrat debate, a choreographed pageant extravaganza, ignored the outside world.

Kamala Harris shot up in the polls with a sound-bite gut punch to

Joe Biden. He had not expected busing to schools decades ago to be a primary issue. She backpedaled days later after he had a chance to answer in more than 60 seconds.

Harris is a polished pit bull in prosecutorial mode, vital in Congress where so many lapdog senators need a chomp in the butt. But a new president has to reverse hostility from allies and enemies with personal integrity earned over time.

A wide field includes some bright promise for the future. For now, in my view, only Biden and Elizabeth Warren have shown enough command of global complexities to steer a foundering ship of state off the rocks. They would make a great team.

In America, alas, running mates are chosen by strategists' assumptions about electability, not for competence. Today, that is risky. Imagine if John McCain had won and died sooner than he did. Sarah Palin is as scary a thought as Mike Pence.

Sports fans who ignore politics saw a thrilling display of America First here in France. Women soccer champs brought home the World Cup to a Manhattan ticker tape parade. Asked if they'd go to the White House, the captain was blunt: No fucking way.

Trump's base is immutable. One should avoid unkind judgments, but Forrest Gump had it right: stupid is as stupid does. Worse are the smart ones, like a former AP technician who offered a new name for the *Mort Report*: I Hate Trump—Read On.

"You used to be known and respected as being a special AP correspondent, a reporter that covered fairly the world," he wrote. "With all due respect, I think you have lost direction… Isn't there something else you can report about?"

True enough, I dislike Trump because I've reported on him occasionally since the 1980s and know him for the heartless thug that he is. I would love to finish those half-finished uplifting dispatches I keep putting aside. This is not personal.

Failing an answer to my reply to him, I can only guess that he is among those who see their investment portfolios soar before the inevitable reckoning when gravity catches up with a doped market and Tariff Man's approach to trade.

People like that are prepared to abandon basic human decency while they hasten the demise of a world headed toward endgame. Trump's administration is not like any we've seen. We all need to bang away to convince the open-minded of what is at stake.

On the national level, a vulgar narcissistic hypocrite enables big money to plunder natural resources and public land, politicize the courts, curb personal freedoms and rig electoral procedures. Beyond our insulating oceans, it is far more than that.

The British ambassador's leaked cable brought this global emergency into focus. He described as inept and erratic a president who immediately showed that was gross understatement. Trump's outrageous tweets define how the world sees America.

Trump heaps praise on Putin, Xi, Kim, and Mohammed Bin Salman, despots who stomp on values Americans profess to believe in. He declares persona non grata our closest ally's envoy for reflecting reality in a secret report to his government.

Nothing illustrates how low we have descended than what is happening on the Mexican border, a symbiotic frontier I have crisscrossed countless times since I was a kid growing up in Tucson.

Democrats don't want an "open border" but rather fences or surveillance that run along its entire length. Drugs come mostly through ports of entry. Smugglers can fly over or tunnel under any new barrier. The Wall is about Trump playing to his base.

Under Barack Obama, some illegal migrants were treated badly when detained, but that pales in comparison to a deliberate policy of forced suffering and family separation or Gestapo-like roundups to scare off desperate families seeking asylum.

Ben Ferencz, who prosecuted Nazis at Nuremburg, calls Trump tactics a crime against humanity. Concentration camps is an apt enough term. Not only reporters but also congressmen are denied access. On supervised visits, only guards are allowed cameras. Some take mocking pictures of elected legislators—their bosses.

Volunteer health workers say they are turned away despite increasing deaths among untreated detainees. Asylum candidates wait months in squalor worthy of those "shitholes" that Trump disparages as the understaffed vetting process creeps along.

One former Homeland Security official made the point after *ProPublica* exposed a closed Facebook group of active and retired border agents: "If you're going to joke about dead Hispanic babies and raping members of Congress on Facebook in front of 9,500 of your colleagues, what are you saying and doing in private?"

A society that cannot trust its lawmen and detention officers is sick to its core. That old question recurs: Why do "they" hate us?

Trump, in character, blames Democrats for the crises he caused and could stop with those executive orders he uses to circumvent checks and balances. He tweets remarks like, "HOAX," when reporters reveal the extent of his cruelty.

More doctors, social workers and immigration judges are essential. Rather than cutting off aid to Central America, Trump can increase it to help struggling farmers and press governments to crack down on violence that forces people to leave home.

The problem is part of larger folly. As human tides inevitably rise around the world, sealed borders make long-term crises worse. In its own self-interest, America needs to do basically the opposite of what Trump is doing.

Health care, racial and gender equality, income distribution are all crucial issues. But, first, someone has to crank down the heat under a world on the boil.

In Ilhan Omar's Somalia

JULY 29, 2019, PARIS - Ilhan Omar might have been one of those hollow-eyed Somali kids at the edge of survival I saw back in the early 1990s, covering humanity's ugly underside for the Associated Press.

The world had ignored foreseeable famine. A warlord despot battled with murderous rivals, all demanding chunks of whatever was left to plunder. Heading inland from Mogadishu, I wrote: "On the blacktop road to Baidoa, a sunbaked corpse lies in the center, the chest emptied by vultures. It might have been a bullet, a bus or hunger. In Somalia, no one stops to find out.

"Scores of thousands have died this year, another 2,000 with every sunrise. A million may follow. But beyond the numbing statistics, the impact comes one death at a time.

"In Baidoa, Amina Sheikh Mohammed, a nurse, stood in the yard of a feeding center and told a visitor that six children had died that day. A man spoke softly in her ear, and her face clouded.

"'Make that seven,' she said."

Omar was born in 1982, the youngest of seven siblings. When she was two, her mother died. After her father, a teacher, saw Somalia falling apart beyond repair, he led the kids on a harrowing trek to spend four years in Dadaab, a hellhole refugee camp in Kenya.

The family made it to New York in 1992 and sought asylum, the way my father's family escaped Russian mayhem in 1921. Omar became a U.S. citizen in 2000, at 17, six years before Melania Trump.

Decent Minnesotans put her in the state legislature. Hijab notwithstanding, she won 78 percent of the vote. After a single term of watching her in action, they sent her to Congress.

It is not likely Ilhan Omar hates her new homeland. And it is no surprise that she reviles Trump, who evokes the sort of ruthless demagogy and blind greed that pushed Somalia into a "shithole."

No one still reading this needs a recap of Trump's cynical jihad against Omar. Yet a close look at how he distorts her words and twists their context shows depraved indifference to truth.

By his criteria, those who cross him don't "love" America and should leave. That includes three other off-white congresswomen who, like Springsteen and a lot of us, were born in the USA.

Unlike most legislators, Omar has learned world reality the hard way, and she says what she sees. She is no more anti-Semitic than Jews who believe Trump's policy threatens Israel's survival.

Israel is a democracy, not a Jewish Vatican. Treating Bibi Netanyahu as a pope stirs global anti-Semitism to an alarming degree. Lots of Israelis want peace with a separate Palestine.

That "Benjamins" remark was slang for the $100 bills that feed an active lobby, with a play on Netanyahu's name. Omar apologized when she realized how it might be misconstrued.

Her use of the word "evil" was directed at overkill response in Gaza and the West Bank. Facts are facts. She applies the same word to Muslim terrorists who pervert Mohammed's teachings.

Omar helps openminded Americans understand how their own foreign policy plays a role in global terrorism, which is essentially an extreme response to perceived injustice.

"No one wants to face how their actions... would have contributed to the rise of terrorism," she said in a thoughtful interview in 2013 after Al-Shabaab attacked a Nairobi mall.

Societies can't be defined by the actions of an unelected few, she said. But in America, a homegrown Christian terrorist is seen as an isolated psychopath. If the perpetrator is Muslim, most people hold all of Islam to account.

This swells terrorist ranks. Frustrated young people react to what they see as unjust American policy and misguided military intervention. Arguing changed nothing. It's their reality, not ours.

Somalia is a telling case.

In 1981, I covered famine after old enmity flared into war on the Ethiopian border. Mogadishu, in contrast, was a placid ex-colonial Italian style city with memorable pasta, parks and beaches where the only worry was great white sharks.

People like Omar's grandfather pushed for democracy and education for women. He was director of National Marine Transport before fishermen-turned-pirates ruled the waves.

Diplomacy and aid might have helped Somalia thrive, but the outside world waited until it was too late to save. My trip in 1992 showed the futility of making peace at gunpoint.

U.S. troops landed in what we called the Frankie Avalon Beach Party. After Pentagon briefers eager for publicity tipped off news editors, generals howled when TV lights lit up commandos sneaking ashore at night. They needn't have worried. Ragtag militias had no desire to confront them head on.

The next morning, I followed a Marine foot patrol from Mogadishu port, bruisers in body armor with heavy weapons. Within an hour, kids dashed out to steal stuff off their packs.

Those kids saw quickly that tough Marines were like ripped weightlifters made impotent by too many steroids. Unless they were willing to gun down civilians, they were all show.

A year later, Somalis shot down a Black Hawk helicopter and dragged a dead crewman through the streets. Bill Clinton pulled out the troops. Then, fearing another debacle, he abandoned Rwanda to the genocide that killed 800,000 people.

As Somalia deteriorated, Washington backed Ethiopian troops, historic foes, to keep order. Al-Shabaab formed to resist them. Today, appropriating the name of Allah, it terrorizes Kenya.

Politics are personal. The Squad unnerves people resistant to change. A lot of others favor exotic spice in the melting pot and would rather see Trump "go back" if he is unhappy with America.

But everyone faces the same looming global calamities. To do the right thing, we need firsthand witnesses like Ilhan Omar to help us see what that is.

"Our House Is on Fire!" (Yawn)

AUGUST 28, 2019, WILD OLIVES, FRANCE - An old *New Yorker* cartoon
has a couple sitting among flowers on a mountainside gazing upon a
see-forever view under sunny skies flecked with wispy clouds. Birds
and butterflies swoop by. And the guy says something like, "The world
is shit."

I get it; I'm even beginning to bore myself. A *Mort Report* meant to
range widely, with stabs at humor, has descended into a one-note
screed about a Machiavellian miscreant back home in America.
Friends of sound mind know better than to invite me to dinner.

True, this is still a pretty good world. Yet in Biarritz beyond the horizon,
President Emmanuel Macron welcomed leaders to the G7 summit
with an alarm-bell tweet: "Our house is on fire!" He meant it literally.

Amazon, for most people these days, evokes Jeff Bezos' empire of books
and canned beans. But in the real Amazon, half the size of Europe,
Brazilian President Jair Bolsonaro is getting away with a crime to end
all crimes: planetary ecocide.

Fires in Brazil to clear land for cattle, crops and timber approach
80,000 since Bolsonaro took power in January—85 percent above last
year's rate. Black smoke turns day to night in São Paulo, thousands
of miles away from the Amazon. In the last eight months, flames
consumed 4.6 million acres of the Brazilian Amazon.

Those figures are from the prestigious National Institute for Space
Research, but new ones will be suspect. Bolsonaro sacked its director
for reporting that fires soared 278 percent in July over the same month
last year, saying he was unpatriotic for damaging Brazil's reputation.

The Amazon emits 20 percent of Earth's oxygen, and it traps carbon.
Waterways it shelters add moisture that keeps it healthy. If this vital
lung were to collapse, scientists calculate, atmospheric damage could
equal what was done over the last 150 years.

At the summit, rich-world leaders pledged $20 million to help fight the fires, only four times more than Leonardo DiCaprio donated on his own. The big dog among them skipped the session on climate change. Donald Trump's aides say he had private talks with Angela Merkel and Narendra Modi who, in fact, were with everyone else at that session.

Bolsonaro tells critics to butt out of Brazil's business. Colonial days are over, he says, and all that land is too valuable to be left to half-naked Indians and do-gooder environmentalists. He has savaged laws, enabling wealthy developers who put him in power to burn and bulldoze.

President Emmanuel Macron welcomed leaders to the G7 summit with an alarm-bell tweet: 'Our house is on fire!' He meant it literally.

When Pope Francis, among others, recently voiced concern, he replied: "Brazil is a virgin that every foreign pervert desires." That raises a crucial question: How much can a domestic pervert in a single country be allowed to defile when an entire planet is struggling to survive?

Bolsonaro has removed so many constraints that Norway and Germany are scrapping a decade-old $1.2 billion conservation project because of his meddling. Brazil's neighbors suffer. Bolivia and Colombia now fight their own fires. Venezuela, near collapse, is otherwise occupied.

Clearing the Amazon diverts waterways. Fewer trees mean less moisture. Crops are impacted across most of the continent. "If Brazil were damming a real river, not choking off an aerial one," The Economist observed, "downstream nations could consider it an act of war."

That is just South America. Forests that have been decimated over recent decades across Africa and Asia are vanishing fast. Countless lost species of flora and fauna might have provided cures for cancer, heart disease or dementia.

Emmanuel Desclaux, a world-class paleontologist at the university in

Nice, has studied climatic ups and downs over the past million years. This time, he said, is different. The Earth's real lungs are its seas, now warming and acidifying so fast that even massive financial aid would be a drop in the ocean. That leaves the forests.

"Nature is resilient, but humans aren't," he told me. "There are too many people now, and we are outstripping the ability to replace oxygen. At some future point, everyone on Earth will suffocate. What troubles me so much is that we are doing this consciously."

Desclaux doesn't venture a guess about when that would happen. But, he said, "It won't be within the political mandate of politicians who will have to answer for it."

Nathaniel Palmer, a *Rolling Stone* reporter on an Antarctic expedition, noted that climate scientists increasingly avoid speaking publicly because so much of the news media gets things wrong. Oversimplifying, he wrote, allows vested interests to sow confusion.

One expert he quoted had a simple response for climate deniers: If you want a demonstration, put a plastic bag over your head and secure it around your neck.

Bolsonaro perseveres with backing from Washington. A tropical Trump, he fires up rallies with bombast. He eased gun laws and extols the days when death-squad militias hunted down dissidents. He once famously told one critic she was too ugly to rape.

Writ large, the Amazon exemplifies Trump's own headlong looting of American wilderness, watersheds, oil and mineral deposits, aquifers, wetlands and coastlines. Former lobbyists and land rapists oversee the government agencies meant to protect them.

U.S. foreign policy no longer pushes the big four "developing" nations, known as BRIC, to protect the environment. The B is Brazil. In Russia, Putin depends on oligarchs who savage ecology for oil and gas. India and China compete to plunder raw materials in poor countries.

"COP"—a U.N. framework meaning conference of the parties—began to confront climate change in 1997. After 20 meetings, the 2016 Paris Agreement offered hope. Then Trump withdrew the United States. Others broke promises. Today, COP-OUT is closer to it.

Beyond climate, the Amazon crisis is an immediate threat to people who have thrived there for at least 13,000 years, living in balance with its ecology. Whole communities are driven off and sometimes tortured by murderous armed gangs with apparent official backing.

Bolsonaro dismisses them as backward sub-humans. But anthropologists say Amazonian tribes devised a precise sun calendar 13,000 years ago. Some migrated north to build an elaborate city at Chaco Canyon in northern New Mexico. Rituals and paintings suggest links to Hopis and Zunis who trace back to Chaco.

Back in 1859, John Stuart Mill argued that responsible nations had a duty to cross borders to protect people suffering from their governments if intentions were moral and not territorial. In recent decades, aid agencies seized on this idea as "humanitarian intervention." As Syria demonstrates, however, this can be devilishly complicated.

Brazil takes this concept to a different level. Bolsonaro flips a finger at the outside world as he amps up plunder that imperils human survival. In a stunning display of ego, he said Brazil would accept G7 funds only if Macron apologized for his "gratuitous" criticism of a sovereign state.

After the summit, he provoked fury with a Facebook exchange. A Brazilian supporter posted a photo meme of his wife next to Brigitte Macron, 27 years older, saying the French president was simply jealous. Bolsonaro wrote (in translation): "Don't humiliate the guy. LOL."

At the closing press conference, Trump skirted a question about whether he still thought climate change was a hoax. He replied with a paean to America's new role as energy superpower and boasted about opening the Alaskan wilderness to oil drilling.

"The United States has tremendous wealth... under its feet," he said. "I've made that wealth come alive." Oil and gas enriched America, he said, and he would not waste that windfall on alternative energy—a "dream." When the reporter pressed for an answer on climate change, Trump turned his back and walked away.

In America, as in the Amazon and everywhere else, that economic wealth under our feet requires stripping away the natural wealth on top. Heedless gluttony racks up immediate profit. But then what?

None So Blind...

OCTOBER 03, 2019, TUCSON, ARIZONA - The scary part of America's descent down a rabbit hole is less the mad ruler who bellows, "Off with their heads!", than so many salt-of-the-earth guys like Tony, my friendly plumber, who accepts his denial of damning evidence that he himself produced.

That Ukraine phone call ought to impact like planes leveling the World Trade Center. Far more destructive than a terrorist attack, it shows an American president undermining democracy at a time when emboldened dictators plunder a world faced with mass extinctions.

Yet Tony tunes out impeachment fervor as just more noise from a corrupt liberal media monolith. "Hillary and Obama did the same thing," he tells me. I don't argue. He's a good guy at heart with an immutable viewpoint: journalists, like plumbers, make a living by stirring up shit.

Donald Trump is gambling that enough people like Tony believe him over their own eyes and ears. History warns us to worry. In the 1500s, a British writer coined a phase that sums up human reality dating back to the Bible: There are none so blind as those who will not see.

In the wider world, allies no longer trust America to do the right thing —or even know what that is. China, Russia and regional powers all over the map are muscling into positions of control. The European Union, bedeviled by its own existential crises, is coming unstuck.

Samantha Power, the Harvard professor and journalist who was Barack Obama's U.N. ambassador, put the Ukraine affair into global perspective in a CNN interview. In sum, she said Trump has crippled America's ability to lead by example.

"The president is blatantly extorting a foreign leader (of) a country that has been invaded by Russia, a country that interfered in our election previously," she said, "and our president is trying to advance his own political welfare rather than look out for an ally."

Power added, "The fact that people put that transcript out and thought it would be somehow helpful for the president I think just speaks to how accustomed the people around President Trump have become to this pattern of behavior."

As impeachment looms, Trump triples down with a tweet storm. He says the mysterious analyst should be hunted down and dealt with summarily. "I'm appalled," former acting CIA director Michael Morell said. "I mean, he's basically saying that this person should be killed."

Trump accused Adam Schiff of treason—a capital offense—for joining other House committee leaders in demanding an investigation to hear testimony. If Congress attempts to check and balance his authority, he warned, it could spark civil war.

He no longer bothers to seek dirt on Joe Biden; he simply invents it. "Biden and his son are stone-cold crooked," he said on Fox News. Even if that were true, against all evidence, it is beside the point. The impeachable crime is involving a foreign country in American elections.

Partisans rallied round like hogs jostling at a trough. Rep. Jim Jordan, an Ohio Republican, told Jake Tapper on CNN, "If Democrats want to impeach because Rudy Giuliani talked to a couple of Ukrainians, good luck with that." After lengthy sparring, Tapper said, "I can't believe you're okay with this." Jordan smirked and kept at it.

Jordan harped on Hunter Biden's board position at a Ukrainian company. Any "what-about" argument pales next to dubious dealings by Trump offspring. One example: *Vanity Fair* reported in 2017 how Eric Trump bragged about $100 million in loans for golf resorts. "We don't rely on American banks," he said. "We have all the funding we need out of Russia."

The Washington Post exposed the report in an editorial and, as they did with Watergate, editors sent reporters to dig. Others joined in. Watergate was a domestic affair, spying on Democrats down the road from the White House. "I am not a crook," Nixon said, but he resigned when it was obvious that he was. Trump's approach is his old standby:

So, sue me.

Trump no longer answers to the people he is sworn to serve. His press secretary is a public-relations shill. Daily briefings are now occasional media performances in which Trump ignores questions and rails against newspapers of record that ferret out wrongdoing.

"China should start an investigation into the Bidens," he told reporters this week with no hint of evidence, "because what happened in China is just about as bad as what happened with Ukraine." This is far beyond Lewis Carroll's Wonderland rabbit hole.

In political rallies, Trump mocks the legislative and judicial process designed to keep watch on the presidency. "They're handing out subpoenas like cookies," he says. "Cookies!" Of course, they are—with reason. And Trump obstructs justice yet further by ignoring them.

Americans—who call their single-nation baseball classic the World Series—obsess on what the impeachment showdown means at home. Meantime, few notice smoldering crises that risk bursting into flame all over the map.

Beyond Iran, North Korea and Israel-Palestine, two old foes with nuclear arsenals—India and Pakistan—face off over Kashmir. Russia, like China, is trying to recolonize much of Africa. Slash-and-burn fires in Indonesia mirror devastation in the Brazilian Amazon.

Trump is hardly responsible for all of these conflagrations, but rather than helping to extinguish them, he is fanning the flames. Dereliction of duty ranks high among his impeachable offenses.

That treacherous self-serving phone call should be enough for an open-and-shut case. But it may not be. Even with so much evidence in plain sight, polls suggest about 45 percent of Americans oppose even an inquiry into whether there are grounds for impeachment.

Maverick Democrats obstruct the process. Congresswoman Rashida Tlaib distributes t-shirts emblazoned, "Impeach the M.F." Clever but not helpful in swaying conservative voters still on the fence.

The Ukraine case supports one clear-cut indictment. Robert Mueller's exhaustive report on Russian meddling directs congressional prosecutors to many more. Although a Republican Senate won't convict, trial in the House can cut through all of Trump's flimflam smokescreens.

"The impeachment power was built for moments like this one," constitutional guru Laurence Tribe wrote in the *Guardian*. "It exists to guard against would-be tyrants who sacrifice democracy and sell out national security... especially when they embroil foreign nations in that corrupt effect." https://bit.ly/3aXOMGq

The House must act quickly and decisively, with a broad range of testimony to shed light on the full extent of Trump's depredations, Tribe added. That would focus wavering voters before elections next year. But don't count on Tony the plumber.

What We Don't Know is Killing Us

OCTOBER 29, 2019, PARIS – Half awake, I hoped it was a jetlag nightmare, but no. Donald Trump was boasting on TV that he alone had made the world safe. And for nearly an hour he splashed kerosene on embers, which America-hating zealots are now likely to fan into flame.

I just returned to the real world after a month in a dis-United States that is today lost in a galaxy of its own. The raid on Abu Bakr al-Baghdadi succeeded in spite of Trump, not because of him, and the worst may be yet to come.

Yes, this is yet more commentary about an over-covered episode. But step back and consider the bigger backdrop.

Too many Americans beyond Trump's hardcore take him at his word. Terrorism, he assures them, is now only Europe's problem. In fact, his ham-handed personal approach to policy swells extremist ranks and alienates essential allies.

And this reflects a cognitive disconnect that suggests Trump may well be reelected despite his flagrant impeachable offenses, abuse of power, enrichment at public expense, divisive partisanship and sociopathic narcissism.

A broad coalition defeated the Islamic State's caliphate, but terrorism is a state of mind, a borderless reaction to perceived injustice. Taunting a revered martyr goads new leaders and loners to seek payback in America, the belly of beast.

The hunt for al-Baghdadi dates back a decade, with relentless pursuit by U.S. intelligence pros who Trump disparages, helped by Kurds and Iraqis he has abandoned. He only gave the order. After playing golf, he alleges to have watched the final act from the White House.

Stumbling over a prepared text, Trump pronounced Abu as "Ah-BOO," which suggests he has ignored briefings by aides familiar with the common Arabic prefix. Then he rambled on with alternative facts, revealing operational details that put future missions at risk.

Given Trump's near-zero credibility, it is open to question whether al-Baghdadi cowered, screamed and whimpered before "he died like a dog." In any case, that humiliating image will enflame ISIS sympathizers from Southeast Asia to Africa and beyond.

As its caliphate began to collapse, ISIS urged freelance disciples to act in its name. An American-born Muslim, for one, killed 14 people and wounded another 22 at a San Bernardino, California, office party in 2015.

Feeding terrorism is only one result of belief in Trump's worldview. In rural America, for instance, people ready to blast a shotgun at drivers who piss them off cheer a leader who undoes democracy and hastens climate chaos that risks making their children's lives unlivable.

The hypocrisy is stunning. Trump excoriates al-Baghdadi for beheading journalists yet lionizes a Saudi prince whose goons dismembered a *Washington Post* columnist. For him, the Middle East is all about oil, as if Russia, Syria and Iran will clear the way for ExxonMobil.

Trump encourages authoritarians to plunder dwindling resources and stamp out human rights, heedless to the inevitable result. But as the Democrat debates make clear, few Americans dwell on confusing global events beyond their line of sight.

Out in the real world, where sweeping existential threats are easily ignored, what we don't know is killing us.

By now, Trump's attempted Ukraine extortion is open-and-shut grounds for impeachment, far worse than charges against Richard Nixon or Bill Clinton. The only question is whether enough Americans care enough to uphold the Constitution.

As crises worsen, unlikely voices urge Americans to think beyond jobs, health care, stock markets and the illusion that strong-arm trade tactics will bring lasting prosperity. "Fake news" is no longer an amusing idiocy from a buffoon president.

One tweet caught my attention: "The White House Trump statement telling the entire Federal Government to terminate subscriptions to the NYT and Wash Post is a watershed moment in national history. No room for HUMOROUS media coverage. This is deadly serious. This is Mussolini."

It was from retired Gen. Barry McCaffrey, the only officer who detained me as a prisoner of war during half a century of reporting. That was a small-bore incident, worth a laugh in hindsight, but it foreshadowed what has since followed.

During the 1991 Gulf War, some of us reporters escaped press pools by eluding checkpoints to find field commanders who welcomed coverage. McCaffrey, I'd been told, was one of them. But when a photographer and I found his outpost near the Iraq border, MPs detained us on orders from headquarters.

We offered to leave; they said they'd shoot if we left before a colonel arrived to chew us out. When he did, I yelled at him, and he let us return to Dhahran. Upon arrival, the Saudi liaison officer told me McCaffrey wanted us thrown out of the country. "But, sir," the Saudi asked him, "what about your First Amendment?"

Since then, the Pentagon has shaped its own reality with televised briefings and strict control on reporters. In the Iraq war, we knew little of prison torture, which fed hatreds that spawned ISIS. Still, we saw U.S. troop behavior that created non-combatant sympathizers.

Barack Obama was open to the press, but he cracked down on leakers. His prosecutors tried long and hard to jail Jim Risen of the *New York Times* for not revealing sources of stories on CIA covert actions. And now Trump, as McCaffrey says, is Mussolini.

White House briefings are over; the press secretary is a shameless shill. The Cabinet, even the attorney general, defends the president from the legislative branch, helped by an increasingly partisan judiciary.

Threats to democracy at home are obvious, happening in plain sight. Elections can undo much of the damage. Out in the real world, where sweeping existential threats are easily ignored, what we don't know is killing us.

Taking out al-Baghdadi was a significant step that shows even a master of clandestine existence is eventually tripped up by disaffected followers, technology and sophisticated forensics. But it hardly signals an end to terrorism, a symptom of something bigger.

For now, it is a tossup. Enough voters may see Trump for who he is and dump him. If not, he will make America yet more cocky, complacent and clueless about why friends turn away—and why so many zealots are prepared to die in acts of vengeance.

IV. WHAT'S GONE IS GONE; NOW WHAT?

Fresh Hope Atop Hell's Backbone

AUGUST 25, 2020, BOULDER, UTAH - Atop Hell's Backbone Road, a spectacular mountain road topretty much nowhere, two of America's better angels see hope for an awakened America with a clear sense of what "great" means.

Up here in crisp piney air, Blake Spaulding and her friend, Jen Castle, show what is possible. But after nearly four years in Trump-polluted purgatory down below, it is clear that recapturing the soul of America will take far more than electoral victories.

"We have to realize that this planet is the best spaceship we could ever have to traverse the cosmos," Blake told me, "and if we don't trash the place, we can have some fun along the way."

True enough. The challenge is beyond a change of leaders. We need to fix America and rejoin a wider world to steer our spaceship planet onto a wiser course. This is our last chance to heed a warning from Justice Louis Brandeis more than a century ago:

"We can have democracy in this country, or we can have great wealth concentrated in the hands of a few. But we can't have both."

Boulder, population near 200 since 1890, was once the most remote settlement in the lower 48 states. Until heroic crews carved a gravel road and bridged a deep gorge in 1933, it was a two-day burro trek from the nearest town. Electricity arrived only in 1947.

Now a paved highway snakes along a narrow spine 29 miles past Escalante above rock sculptures that reach to the horizons. It's not for the faint-hearted. Icy winter snow or a badly handled curve can send you hurtling down 1,500 feet on either side.

Blake and Jen pitched up in 2000 after catering raft trips down

Colorado River rapids in Arizona. Boulder lived mostly Old West-style, heavy on beans and beef. Soon, devotees drove days to bump elbows with locals around the fire at their Hell's Backbone Grill.

Dishes like "dreamy creamed Swiss chard" and Buddhist prayer flags at first befuddled conservative Mormon families whose forebears pioneered the place. But Blake and Jen made friends fast, and they got a liquor license for a well-stocked bar and wine cellar.

They added a six-acre farm to produce 160 crop varieties on impossible high-desert soil: fields of staple grains, gardens of exotic greens, and trees bursting with fruit. Along with an online shop, they kept an energized Boulder buzzing.

The grill closed in 2020 before Covid-19 could find its way up Hell's Backbone. Now the menu, including The Dinner Jenchilada, is takeout or served on the patio. Indoor dining will likely return, but much of the wilderness splendor around it may be soon be gone.

In one of his last acts, Barack Obama established the Grand Staircase-Escalante National Monument. A year later, Donald Trump cut its 2,000 square miles by half and slashed 85 percent off Bears Ears National Monument, Bill Clinton's legacy across the mountain. Blake joined environmentalists to block the decision in court. A lawsuit is pending. Meantime, prospectors, ranchers and developers are moving in with plans that would obliterate ancient Native American ruins on land sacred to a dozen Indian tribes.

Utah exemplifies the reality of Trump's repeated boasts about streamlining regulatory bureaucracy. That guts the EPA, the U.S. Forest Service, the Army Corps of Engineers and agencies that have protected water, air, biodiversity and wildlife for generations.

An executive order in July weakened the 50-year-old National Environmental Policy Act to limit public review of government permits. It followed 100 rollbacks of federal rules, which are badly needed as climatic changes wreak increasing havoc.

Conservationists and Indian tribes have kept much of the plunder at bay in courts. But another four years of Trump would destroy rich heritage from the Alaskan wilds to Florida coastlines.

National monuments, unlike parks, are multiuse; local authorities are required to hear public comment, but nothing defines how. Early in 2017, Blake rose at dawn and drove two hours to be first in line for a hearing at the Garfield County seat of Panguitch. Known to be articulately outspoken, she was excluded from the few allowed to speak for a measured minute. In Boulder, when I asked what she would have said, she made her minute count:

"We are ever more disconnected as our society's pace accelerates and mechanizes. The only way we can remember we are human animals is to spend time in nature, to delight in actual quiet, hear bird songs and become friends with plants. If we need this now, in 50 years when I'm long gone, we will need it way more." Grand Staircase-Escalante, she said, shelters 665 distinct species of wild bees, a crucial component of its ecology. That's one example. When you tear out chunks of nature's elaborate web, expect eventual calamity.

"There are endless reasons to save it, and the reason to destroy it is for outdated fossil fuel and minerals," she concluded. "We are strip mining our planet, our mother. We have a responsibility to save it for future generations and to do right by contemporary indigenous people."

When Trump savaged the two monuments, then Interior Secretary Ryan Zinke told reporters, "This is not about energy." He denied repeatedly that mining was planned. But the area is rich in coal deposits. And Energy Fuels Resources (USA), America's only uranium processing plant, sits just outside of Bears Ears.

The Washington Post obtained documents that debunked Zinke's alternative facts. The American subsidiary of a Canadian company had lobbied hard for more land to allow easier access for radioactive ore. Andrew Wheeler, its chief lobbyist, now runs the EPA.

Theodore Roosevelt signed the Antiquities Act of 1906, used 100 times by presidents to designate national monuments or protect land with "significant natural, cultural or scientific features." It is not clear whether later presidents can rescind that protection.

But Trump bulls ahead. From Interior Secretary David Bernhardt on down, he has appointed lawyers and lobbyists who before joining government worked hard to open public land for private use. And official spin misleads much of the electorate.

Headlines hailed the bipartisan Great American Outdoors Act, which Trump just signed into law. Essentially, it only replaces funds approved in 1965 to maintain national parks that were diverted elsewhere over the years.

Senators Cory Gardner of Colorado and Steve Daines of Montana, fighting to keep popular Democrats from taking their seats, pushed the bill. Environmentalists liked it, but ranchers and agribusiness didn't. Trump signaled he would veto it.

Gardner, visiting the White House, pointed to a portrait of Teddy Roosevelt and played on Trump's vanity. The bill would allow him to emulate a beloved Republican who championed the great American outdoors. "Put it on my desk," Trump said.

Mitch McConnell reluctantly plucked the bill from his dead-letter pile, badly in need of those Senate seats. Trump affixed his signature with great fanfare, declaring himself to the greatest environmental president in more than a century.

In fact, Trump's hit list for opening public land to coal mines, oil drilling, and other private exploitation amounts to more than 13 million acres, nearly the size of West Virginia. He has yet more plans to entrench an oligarchy that allows him free rein.

Robert Reich's slim tome, *The System: Who Rigged It, How We Fit It*, exudes hope. The key, he writes, is waking up voters to just how badly democracy has been crippled. In 2016, the richest one-hundredth of 1 percent of Americans accounted for 40 percent of campaign contributions. That bought a tax cut, which increased the federal debt by $1.9 trillion. Next to nothing trickled down. Stock buybacks sent the Dow soaring.

"The problem is not excessive greed," he wrote. "If you took the greed out of Wall Street, all you'd have left is pavement. The problem is the Street's excessive power."

Senators raise tens of millions for a job that pays $174,000 a year. Half work as lobbyists when they leave office. In one passage, Reich quotes Trump in 2016: "'I give money to everybody, even the Clintons, because that's how the system works.'" To which Reich adds, "Those might have been the most honest words ever to come out of his mouth."

Countless examples, from reprehensible to outrageously corrupt, show staggering unjust inequality. Poor people lose homes for a missed payment. Taxes bail out corporations that lose multiple billions. CEOs make 300 times their worker's wages.

One answer is graduated taxes, as in all other wealthy nations. For the über-rich, money is how you keep score. For those living week to week, it is no game. America's richest 0.01 percent—160,000 households— owns as much as the bottom 90 percent. The poorest half of the nation controls just 1.3 percent of its wealth.

Amazon paid no income tax for two years. Its 2019 bill was 1.2 percent of a $13.1 billion net profit. That year, Jeff Bezos joined 180 CEOs of the Business Roundtable to pledge fairness to all stakeholders, employees and customers included. Weeks later, Whole Foods cut health benefits to part-time workers, saving what Bezos earns in two hours. Another answer is cutting through bullshit. The book is framed as a reply to Jamie Dimon, who was stung when Reich criticized him. Dimon said he was a patriot before being CEO of JPMorgan, a Democrat who did much for the impoverished. Yes, Reich agreed, but he is also dangerously deluded.

"Socialism," Dimon wrote in his 2019 letter to shareholders, "inevitably

produces stagnation, corruption and often worse—such as authoritarian government officials who often have an increasing ability to
interfere with both the economy and individual lives—which they
frequently do to maintain power."

Was he listening to himself? Big money is about profit only for shareholders and huge risks guaranteed by the public treasury. In short,
corporate socialism. Capitalism is for proletariats. Social democracy,
hardly a Soviet gulag, is simply a fairer capital economy.

When Adam Neumann dreamed up WeWork as an office-sharing
company in 2010, JPMorgan lent him enough to buy buildings but
also a $60 million jet, large estates in Westchester County and the
Hamptons, a $27 million Bay Area home and a fancy Manhattan resi-
dence, along with toys like a quarter-million-dollar Maybach car.

WeWork lost $2 billion in 2018. Neumann was forced out before
an IPO in late 2019 with a $1.7 billion severance package and a $46
million a year job as consultant. Thousands of employees faced layoffs,
compensated by worthless stock options.

Reich's book skirted the big question: How much time is left to fix
America? Fierce lightning ignites drought-stressed forests. Flames en-
gulf much of California, reaching 1,000-year-old redwoods, and smoke
chokes its cities. Inland hurricane-force storms devastated 10 million
acres of corn and soybean in Iowa. It will get worse.

Climate barely came up at the Republican Convention, a downer to
a party that pushes fossil fuels for immediate profit. The Democrats
were flayed for wanting to kill jobs with their Green New Deal.

Speakers reduced reality to a party game, whacking a distorted piñata
labeled as the Democrats' platform. Rep. Matt Gaetz of Florida reflected the tone: "They'll disarm you, empty the prisons, lock you in
your homes and invite MS-13 to live next door."

Convention absurdity at times overloaded the Twittersphere with
mockery. Kimberley Guilfoyle, Don Trump Jr.'s girlfriend, delivered

an unhinged rant, so strident that *Mother Jones* added North Korean martial music as background.

Trump claimed he inherited a failing economy, near recession. In fact, Obama reversed George W. Bush's actual recession; his growth rates outperformed Trump's. For now, Trump has pumped-up the stock markets. But he can't repeal the law of gravity.

Over and over, Trump boasted about jobs. Yet he let Covid-19 run wild in America while praising Xi Jinping for effective action to curb the pandemic. Obama left an unemployment rate of 4.7 percent. It is now 10.2 percent.

Trump now flays China, an all-purpose scapegoat. It sent a deadly plague to America, but he has done everything right to beat back "the China virus." Our economy is roaring back as never before, and we are the big dog again. Really? Look around.

Trump's global narrative is an easy sell. With so many crises at home, few Americans look beyond our insulating oceans. The threat is not world war but rather countless unstoppable small ones. And now, more than missiles, the danger is microbes.

South Korea reported its first case on the same day as the United States. By late August, 310 Koreans had died. We will be lucky if our death toll is under 300,000 by November. Other countries tested and traced. Everyone else masked up. We did it all wrong.

Xi admitted the threat in January. He shared research, airlifted aid to the United States and assumed the lead role at the WHO that America abandoned.

Trump's policies have spurred China to begin reshaping the world in its own image: harshly authoritarian, with no regard for cultural diversity, human rights, free expression. It plunders the world for resources by corruption and coercion.

And there is Russia. Trump brushed aside the Republican-controlled bipartisan Senate Intelligence Committee report on Russian meddling in the 2016 election, released only weeks earlier, which detailed his long courtship of Vladimir Putin.

Its nearly 1,000 pages went far beyond the Mueller Report with intimate details of links to Russian intelligence and dirty tricks. But it stopped short of specifying a coordinated campaign. Republicans reduced it all to two words: No collusion.

Putin now has free rein in an unruly world. If Trump did not react to intelligence that Russia had placed a bounty on American troops in Afghanistan, he sees no limits.

Now Trump wants a Nobel Prize ("Noble" in one of his tweets) denied him when his unrequited love affair with Kim Jong-un made a bad situation worse. He brokered a deal in the unholy land: diplomatic ties linking the United Arab Emirates with Israel.

Bibi Netanyahu promised only a temporary halt to settlements in Palestine to save his job. The UAE expects F-35 stealth fighters, a windfall for Lockheed Martin, which would threaten not only Iran but also endanger Israel's aerial dominance in the region.

That could be the straw that finally breaks the camel's back, inflaming the Middle East.

Up on Hell's Backbone, Blake Spaulding had no illusions about what America faces beyond protecting wilderness and natural beauty. "In practice," she said, "we have a lawless administration. So much of it is horrendous, world-destroying, soul-crushing."

But, in her better-angel mode, she exudes hope that enough Americans will stand up and take action. Voting, she says, is the basic minimum. People need to defend what matters to them and join others for a larger purpose.

With time on their hands, Blake and Jen began circulating "A Love Letter From Helles," their little community's newsletter. It includes a quote from Jane Goodall, now 86, who knows about primate societies, from chimpanzees to humans:

"You cannot get though a single day without having an impact on the world around you. What you do makes a difference, and you have to decide what kind of difference you want to make."

V. MORT REPORT MISCELLANY

Dear Incredible

MARCH 31, 2020

Mr. President,

I realize it is unusual for you to receive a letter from a word in the English language, but we self-respecting adjectives can't take much more of your semi-literate babble. Each of us has served a specific purpose to convey singularity, the basic purpose of sophisticated lexicons since Antiquity. My colleague, Tremendous, is miffed at being constantly misused. Our beloved descriptor, Beautiful, is falling about laughing. Poor Perfect is on suicide watch. We haven't been able to locate Bigly or Yuge for comment. As for me, I am livid to the core.

During your recent daily campaign rallies, disguised as coronavirus press briefings, I seem to be every third word out of your mouth. In every other sentence, you assert that I am the proper adjective to define how great (Great, by the way, sends thanks for so much exposure) a job you are doing. That devalues my import and impact down to zero.

Please understand, I have been in regular usage since the 15th century, dating back to the Latin incredibilis. Webster captures my meaning closely enough: "Too extraordinary and improbable to be believed." In truth, my only proper usage in your case is to define the fact that a large, fairly educated nation has chosen you as its leader and has yet to rid itself of you.

Finally, can't you please find someone on your swollen staff of sycophants who can put us words into complete sentences for you? Clarity matters even when, as usual, you are twisting truth. Americans need to know with whom they are dealing. Remember what Joyce Carol Oates observed decades ago: Words are all we have to stand between us and the darkness.

Sincerely,

Incredible

A Note to the Most Dangerous
Man on Earth

APRIL 04, 2018

Dear B.H.,

I know you're no deplorable. You were kind when I visited Idaho in
the '80s and saw the fruits of your successful life. You've taken pains
to explain to me why you support Donald Trump. So I say this with all
respect: You are the most dangerous man on earth.

Not actually, which is why I use the initials of a hapless character in
Aldous Huxley's *Brave New World*: Benito Hoover. Uncork some Snake
River Valley red, gaze upon your splendid ranch, and consider this
note meant as news analysis, not insult.

You told me Trump wasn't perfect, "just 100 times better than Hillary,"
and sent me a link to a loony website that posited "the brain might be
wired differently for liberals and conservatives to explain how they
look at things so differently."

Conservative and liberal? Two one-word labels for 320 million
Americans? You're smarter than that. A lot of honest reporters risk
their lives out in a complex world so that voters like you can make
nuanced, informed judgments based on hard reality.

Still, you wrote, "We will never convince each other so why worry. If I
could leave you with one thought it would be this: When Obama was
elected we feared the very worst, and we weren't wrong. But we didn't
try and sabotage him."

Oh, please. Bias colors perceptions, but facts are black and white.
(Double entendre intended.) Obama reversed George W. Bush's mess,
despite a Republican stone wall. Relaxed borders and trade accords
buoyed the global economy. Rising employment predated Trump.

You asked, "What if even more Americans think lower taxes aren't so bad after all and some draining of the swamp could be a good thing. The Left and the media won't buy it but it seems their credibility is going down the toilet."

That's the trouble. You may be right. Roseanne redux shows a broad fringe of Americans are happy to pretend there is no world beyond our borders, that a temporary burst of irrational exuberance will spare excruciating, increasing pain once reality bites.

Benito Hoover evokes a parade-loving Fascist and a president whose closed mind sank us into the Great Depression. Think back to the 1980s, when we met. That's when Neil Postman foresaw the future in his book, *Amusing Ourselves to Death.*

He wrote: "What Orwell feared were those who would ban books. What Huxley feared was that there would be no reason to ban a book, for there would be no one who wanted to read one. Orwell feared those who would deprive us of information. Huxley feared those who would give us so much that we would be reduced to passivity and egotism.

"Orwell feared that the truth would be concealed from us. Huxley feared the truth would be drowned in a sea of irrelevance. Orwell feared we would become a captive culture. Huxley feared we would become a trivial culture, preoccupied with some equivalent of the feelies, the orgy porgy, and the centrifugal bumblepuppy."

Huxley was wrong about easy sex. Now only our president gets away with boasting about pussy-grabbing. Otherwise, he pegged it perfectly: a people freed of disturbing memory or critical thought focused on amusement and mindless consensus.

In sum, as Christopher Hitchens wrote later, "For true blissed-out and vacant servitude, you need an otherwise sophisticated society where no serious history is taught."

The Soviet Union, an Orwellian dystopia, broke before it bent.

Vladimir Putin, a Huxleyan, feigns democracy at home while undermining it in America with what Lenin called "useful idiots" in Washington and closed minds in the heartland. He hates Hillary Clinton because she understood his new Evil Empire, and pushed back.

In the '80s, as Neil Postman did his research, the Kochs began crippling our education, helped by Ronald Reagan's reverse Robin Hood approach of taking from the poor to give to the rich. Today, we see the result.

America cannot survive, much less thrive, in isolation. We do not get to define how others see us. Your misguided partisans only make them scorn us or hate us. As for the Trump Bump-now-Slump, have you checked your brokerage account this week?

"Benito Hoover" says it all. The world saw Mussolini as a preening petty tyrant, deluded by narcissism. It did not end well for him. Herbert Hoover had lots to brag about as Wall Street soared after his Inauguration. That, remember, was at the beginning of 1929.

You bolster your case with two "foreign" examples:

—"(Trump's) tough talk on Mid-East peace and recognizing Jerusalem as the Capital of Israel didn't start a war and may be positive in bringing people to reality… What if his Jewish son-in-law actually helps bring factions together in the region?"

—"What if our blustery President could startle "little rocket man" to want to talk? Oh, that may now be happening."

Provoked Israeli troops gunning down Gaza rock throwers hardly portends peace. Remember, it was once David who only had stones? As a reporter inconveniently named Rosenblum, I've watched the unholy land fester since the 1960s. Now heavily armed militias and an infuriated populace respond as expected to Trump's political pandering. Be very worried.

Korea? Trump has given Kim Jong-un the status he craves. Let's bet on whether he spikes his nukes. Unless John Bolton outdoes himself for craziness, China will defuse a war it hardly wants. And that will cement its role as the new big dog.

The real problem is why friends and foes alike hold us in such contempt. They see Americans like you make excuses for a man who revels in others' pain, lies outrageously, and bows to the swamp rats he reviled during his campaign.

As you say, I will never convince you. That's not my purpose. This is another reminder from an old-crocodile correspondent that democracy can no longer be a spectator sport.

When we met, Mitch McConnell was just another narrow-minded senator backing Central American tyrants, defending "freedom-fighters" who trafficked drugs in CIA aircraft and caused so many people caught in the middle to seek refuge up north.

Today, smug in his encrusted place at the public trough, he rallied his party to block a perfectly balanced Supreme Court nominee. Trump sold his snake oil. Too many sat out the elections or shunned the woman you say is 100 times worse than what we've got.

Checks and balances is not about who writes checks from their outsized balances. The America presidency is about character and integrity. Congress answers to the people, not a party. Okay, sorry, now I'm sermonizing. But, please, check my facts.

You helped pioneer northern Idaho when its rivers and forests were pristine, when the Indians who preceded us were taken into account. Yet you champion a regime that is destroying wilderness and Native American cultures for immediate profit.

I'm down near the southern border, where Mexicans have had "Americans" attached with a hyphen for eight generations. If you think that insane Wall will stop "aliens" or stem the drug traffic that began booming in the '80s, come down and see for yourself.

We can curb immigration by helping others live better where they'd rather be, at home. We can combat drugs by enriching our own kids with better education, accessible health care and a larger slice of good old American pie.

At one point, you said about Obama, "In fact, we prayed for him, if you can believe it." I can. But I also know the billions on our planet worship a lot of different Gods and gods, with values that extend beyond themselves alone.

Even if you think we should be "first," we can't be a society that that would disgust Christ, Mohammed, Buddha, or I'itoi, the Tohono O'odham's Creator. America is not about some people getting to earn more now at the expense of everyone's children.

Damn, I'm preaching again. I'll leave you with Tom Russell's apolitical little ditty, "Who's Gonna Build Your Wall?" It is Mexican-accented but depicts a universal theme that Benito Hoover would recognize. Here are a few lines and a link:

"As I travel around this big, old world, there's one thing that I fear,
"It's a white man in a golf shirt, with a cellphone in his ear."

https://www.youtube.com/watch?v=LZkAoosVLkA

AN UPDATE: *I am desperate to commune with my oldest, most trusted source, but Emiliano the olive tree doesn't do zoom. And I'm planted in Arizona until the plague subsides. My trees in Provence warned of climate collapse long before anyone did much about it. I wrote this piece in December 2017. Donald Trump spurned the Paris Accords, which had finally focused world attention on impending global calamity. For him, it was a Chinese hoax, just as he later blamed China for his inaction against Covid-19. Olive trees have seen it all and survived it all. On the course we humans are on, we'll be gone before they are.*

Olea Dixit: Olive Trees Know

DECEMBER 06, 2017, WILD OLIVES, FRANCE – Each year about now I return here among old friends to check on the state of the world. Emiliano, Julio, Ernesto, Shithead and the gang have been on watch for centuries. Their Mediterranean roots go back 10 millennia.

Some are now near despair, and a few are fighting for their lives.

Olive trees can't actually talk (and I'm not yet unhinged), but I learn more from them about what matters in the long term than from that fancy Samsung TV blaring away inside my old stone house.

They tell it straight without sponsors and ratings to worry about, or clueless editors guessing at a distance what their message should be. Having been around since before the Bible was a rough draft, their forte is historical continuum.

The trees' immediate grief is the climate chaos that an American president denies. It hasn't rained in seven months. Olives survived, but not most of the genets—broom—that perfume the hills in summer with delicate golden flowers.

Heat and drought fended off the dreaded dacus, the olive fly that last year left the neighborhood without a crop. That was a freak attack, worsened by a new bug and old bacteria that settled into holes bored in the olives. Next year, who knows?

Stepping back, there is a broader message. Nature, like human events, is not determined by what we want it to be or think it is. It takes its course, and we can only mitigate the consequences—or suffer them.

Scientists measure data; trees and crops show us reality. For decades, the late Lester Brown at WorldWatch tracked growing global grain demand and precarious supply. When that balance tips the wrong way, humans go hungry. And in a crunch, food goes not to those who can buy it but rather those who can take it.

• • •

Today, the news is that Donald Trump is moving the U.S. embassy to Jerusalem, which his partisans say has always been Jewish. Those surviving old-timers on the Mount of Olives know history is far more complex than that.

Olives have loomed large in my periodic reporting trips to the unholy land since the 1960s. In 1994, I met Ahmed Nasser, a 38-year-old electrical engineer, a U.S. citizen from Warren, Ohio, who had moved back to his family home in Nablus.

"The olive has deep, deep roots in the ground," he told me, "and we feel that our roots are as deep. The Israelis know this. If anyone throws a stone from a field, they push all the trees off. We get punished for 1,000 years." When Jewish settlers want to claim new territory, he added, they uproot old groves and plant new trees to mark possession.

Feelings are so intense, Nasser said, that Palestinians killed a merchant near Nablus who sold his orchard to Jews who planned to settle.

There is no moral to this story. Each "news" item from Israel and Palestine has 50 shades of grim. Such judgments as right or wrong are up for dispute. But, as always, facts are facts. Nearly a quarter century later, olives remain at the heart of intractable crises that demand serious diplomacy, not donor-pleasing ideology.

Every sign suggests a move would paralyze chances for peace, fortify Iran-backed militants, infuriate many Muslims and further isolate

America. A Brookings poll found 63 percent of U.S. respondents
oppose it. But Trump knows his audience.

· · ·

I named my half-dozen acres in the Provence back hills Wild Olives
because it was such a tangled jungle that I couldn't see the trees for the
forest. After a decade of hard labor, it was tamer, but the name still fit.
In French, it is pronounced like huile d'olive.

In between reportages on war and peace around the world, I return
whenever I can to ponder perspective on "breaking" news. Each year—
each month, now—the abyss widens between what I see out in the real
world and what I hear on that blaring box inside the house.

Ironically, good reporting is better than ever, with courageous, incisive
and often dangerous work. The wondrous web brings us images, data,
links and speed we old hands never imagined. But, ironically, most
Americans have never been so badly informed at a time when a clear
picture of the world is essential to survival.

The problem is that there is too much, too often. Excellent reporting
is lost among clueless guesswork and panel-babble. Finding it takes
sustained attention, crosschecking sources and attention to crucial
nuances as well as big pictures.

Down here, those nuances run to truffles. Life's little pleasures rarely
reach the heights of a freshly found tuber melanosporum grated over
egg noodles in butter with a light splash of hot-off-the-press Provence
olive oil.

I just went to nearby Aups, where a few olive trees date back to the
Romans, for the first truffle market of the season. The few on offer cost
close to a thousand dollars a kilo, which is twice last year's price.

A second-generation producer named Sabine slipped me a fragrant
muddy lump, which her noble hound had found along the roots of
an oak.

"For the past few years, we've had to water around the trees," she said. "Without that, not a chance." Nearby, an old guy in a flat wool cap shook his head. When he was young, he said, pigs in the neighborhood snuffled up a ton a month.

True, a life without truffles hardly matches fallout from a nuclear war accidentally triggered by two unbalanced leaders in a shoving match. The lesson, however, is the same. Quickly or slowly, what we don't know is killing us.

To That Clueless Killer Across the Room:

A friend just told me about her 90-year-old grandmother who refuses to wear a mask; she doesn't want to be mistaken for a Democrat. True enough. Others impose fines for ignoring Covid-19. But it's our right to expose others to painful suffering with a fair chance of dying alone, waving goodbye to loved ones from behind glass.

For you, I'm guessing that it's not about party politics, just partying. It's fun to crowd around a table with friends, tossing back shots with raucous laughter at a social distance of six inches. (But I doubt you'll get lucky with that blonde; she makes a mocking face behind your back.)

My wife and I noticed your condescending smirk at us, about the only ones besides waiters with faces covered. That was at least discreet, unlike the guy I just saw on video who threatened to punch out masked shoppers in a big store for being fools. Didn't they know this is all a hoax?

I get it. We've dumbed down our schools since the 1980s. Two oceans insulate us from the real world. "Me" is today's predominant pronoun. But if your personal freedom means more than protecting others, consider for a moment how this affects you.

Forget about your passport. The Trump virus imprisons us within our borders, banned from 166 countries, including Mexico, Canada and most of Europe. If you could get to Paris, say, forget about jamming into Bastille bars or squeezing melons at Alma market. But it's much worse than that. Americans are outcasts, pitied if not scorned, for handing their keys to a self-obsessed madman, whose crude belligerent policies and climate denial imperil their own future.

Not to profile, but you exude the confidence of a guy who has grown up convinced that we are the big dog, immutably number one. But if Trump cheats his way to reelection, allies will find new trade patterns. China will thwart human rights and muzzle dissent across most of the world. It won't come to war, most likely. It doesn't have to. The Chinese have nukes, too, but and won't risk mutual radioactive destruction. They can afford to wait.

Indulge some advice from a reporter who has watched us lose so much of what was nobly inspiring and decent. We often screwed up, but we tried to do the right thing. To do that, Americans need to know what the right thing is. Read real newspapers and help them survive.

Study history, ancient and modern. It is repeating itself now with frightening permutations. Think about all the human warmth and interaction that we began to lose long before Covid-19.

This goes way beyond the subject of masks. Even if inadvertently, you and your friends are helping a deviant president destroy America and make our planet unlivable for your own kids. In November, please seize what may be our last chance to get on a track back to greatness.

Respectfully,

That old guy at the takeout counter

A Final Word

The Mort Report is hardly just me. It started when Richard Beban, a fallen friend, urged me to turn my occasional email blasts and Facebook bitching into something more. After leaving the Associated Press, freed of bosses' constraints, I had enough squirreled away to pursue projects that matter with pals from the road who share my point of view. Reporting is a profession, but it is also a calling. Lifers don't retire. We're old crocs, hopefully with no "k," who cruise the swamps to take a chomp out of any noxious creatures we find. We don't need no stinking badges—or salaries. But plane tickets, libel lawyers and whatnot add up fast.

Two old friends, Peace Sullivan and Nick Ludington, offered initial wherewithal. Kind reader donations keep us afloat. Sylvana Foa, among the best of old crocs, volunteered to edit copy. Mike Ruby, Merrill McLoughlin and Mike Tharp, pros all, joined in. Jeannette Hermann, my wife, reads everything first and dares to speak her mind. Stalwarts include Phil Cousineau, Alan Weisman, Willis Barnstone and Lito Tejada-Flores, all literary genii. Barbara Gerber, Jim Mitchell and Pepper Provenzano helped make this book happen. Brad Miller watches my back. Geri Thoma, my agent, excuses money-losing conscience projects. Elaine and Bill Petrocelli of Book Passage always champion my work.

Dawn Shepherd produces the Report with skill and enthusiasm. Jeff Danziger, whose sharper wit has skewered bad guys for decades, con-tributed his cartoons. Jacqueline Gilman turned all the stuff I threw at her into this book.

I owe inexpressible thanks to Jacqueline Sharkey, a giant among us, who brought me back to Tucson briefly each year to teach at the University of Arizona. She is a pioneer of guerrilla journalism, break-ing old molds but with a fierce commitment to the often-forgotten essential ethics and tenets of our profession. This book is her idea.

As Trump might say, *The Mort Report* is what it is. "Blog" sounds to me like a cow choking on a salty rag. Newsletter? Not really. These are dispatches, facts gathered at first hand with analysis and context from a long life on the road. Basically, they're reports from a guy named Mort. Sign up for emails at www.mortreport.org. They are free, aimed at a wide reach. But there is a Donate tab on the site if you'd care to join in. If you do, thanks.

Mort Rosenblum has reported on war and peace for 58 years. He went to Africa for Associated Press in 1967, then covered Vietnam and roamed Asia before moving to Argentina at the start of its "dirty war." After a year at the Council on Foreign Relations, he went to Paris as AP

bureau chief, then editor of the *International Herald Tribune*. AP named him special correspondent in 1981 to cover major stories around the world, including Bosnia, Somalia, two Iraq wars and Afghanistan. Independent since 2005, he travels from bases in Paris and Provence, with regular trips to his home in Baja Arizona. His 13 books range from the best-selling *OLIVES*, a James Beard winner, to a journalism textbook on journalism and reportage of international affairs. He has written for the *New York Times, Foreign Affairs*, the *New York Review of Books, Harper's, Le Nouvel Observateur, Monocle* and *Bon Appetit*, among others. He directed an award-winning series for the International Consortium of Investigative Journalists on looting the seas. (A proposed book, *Odious Beast: Confessions of a Newshound*, never made it into print; his agent at the time didn't like dogs.) www.mortrosenblum.net.

CPSIA information can be obtained
at www.ICGtesting.com
Printed in the USA
FSHW020729260920
74154FS